T0209139

The MAKING of a
Queen
A Treasure to Find

DANIELLE KAMDEU

WESTBOW
PRESS®
A DIVISION OF THOMAS NELSON
& ZONDERVAN

WestBow Press books may be ordered through booksellers or by contacting:

WestBow Press
A Division of Thomas Nelson & Zondervan
1663 Liberty Drive
Bloomington, IN 47403
www.westbowpress.com
1 (866) 928-1240

ISBN: 978-1-9736-9344-4 (sc)
ISBN: 978-1-9736-9345-1 (e)

Print information available on the last page.

WestBow Press rev. date: 09/22/2020

Contents

Acknowledgments

I would like to first acknowledge and give glory to Our Lord and Savior Jesus Christ, the Holy Spirit and the Father for giving me this great opportunity and privilege to write this book. I am overwhelmed in all humbleness and gratefulness to acknowledge my depth to the spirit of God who helped me to put these ideas into something concrete. I could not have imagined it possible looking at my own understanding.

But I cannot fail to also express my sincere gratitude and acknowledge the great participation and assistance of the following people:

Apostle Brilliant Efon, who was there from day one to encourage me in this project even when I didn't believe it was possible and he followed up in the writing process, Rev. Kofi Yeboah, my mentor, my Pastor who believed in me even when he barely knew me. He teaches me how to remain a woman after God's heart.

Pastor Annita Achebodt, my sister, my friend, my counsellor who supported me morally and spiritually.

Pastor Rose-Diaz Piquant (I call her my "bulldozer partner").

Mr. Christian Tchameni, Ms. Cecile Kela and Mr Steven Myrthil. You have all assisted me so kindly.

I am extremely grateful to my parents for their encouragements, continuing support, love and prayers; Mrs. Agnes Jojo Pangoua and Ms. Solange Djuitchang I love you both dearly.

To all my relatives and friends who believed in me and to the Westbow Press team, I am grateful.

Thanking you all for your support.

Foreword

There was no hesitation when I was asked to write a foreword to this book. I can say without a shadow of a doubt that Danielle exemplifies the very essence of this book, emphasizing on self-worth and importance to true identity in God. When I first met Danielle and as a member of Life Renewal Charismatic Church (LRCC Ministries), I have seen the uniqueness of personality and the drive to stand out. Her passion for women to discover their true identity and not just to follow the crowd runs through the theme of her speech. I see this passion is woven to the fabric of this book to be very engaging from the beginning; from dealing with questions and misconceptions of the making of the queen in this day and age surface ideology of beauty. I recommend this book to everyone, most especially women and even women ministry groups. As I read the book one thing stood out to me *"It's when you realize that you are living in sin and you are tired of that life, you come to Christ, and then you discover that, in fact, you were like the eagle among chickens; at that moment you will need to leave that chicken yard and decide to be trained as the eagle that you are. It is when you get to know the King that you discover the princess in you."* I can say the training of the eagle becomes the making of the queen.

Rev. Kofi O. Yeboah

Introduction

We were all born princesses. No matter the conditions in which we were born, we were all born princesses.

Somebody will now ask me, "Do you really understand the meaning of this statement? Do you know the struggles that people are going through?" And my answer will be, "Yes, yes I know." But again, I say we were all born princesses. Whether you were born in the poorest home, born out of a rape, or were an unwanted child, whether you were abandoned or rejected or lost both parents at your birth, you were born a princess.

A princess because the Maker of all the universe is the King, who knew you even before the world were created. A King who doesn't make mistakes and is not unfair but is a just judge. Royalty is in the air he breathes, and the earth is his footstool. He is the Father of all nations.

However, we were not all born queens. We choose to become one. And this comes with a need of transformation, a need of change, a need of molding, a need of building. And that is the process that we don't want or like to go through. It's painful, it's demanding, it hurts, and it can hurt so bad. I mean really bad.

The making of a queen is a process. It takes time.

- Time to acknowledge that you are on the wrong way.
- Time to turn away and decide not to go back.

- Time to allow yourself to be broken so that you'll be rebuilt.
- Time to cherish and nurture a relationship.
- Time to hear and obey.
- Time to sacrifice.
- Time to make mistakes and stand up.
- Time to trust and to be betrayed.
- Time to be healed and restored.
- Time to learn and to love.

In brief, it takes time.

Being a queen comes with a lot of responsibilities, including decision-making and disciple-building. It requires a woman, a strong woman and not girl.

But we're usually princesses who decide to stay at the level of being a princess. Nothing wrong with being a princess, but at a certain level of this life, it's either you overtake or you are overtaken. To overtake you'll need to walk in the full authority of a queen, while a princess is limited.

1

Who Is a Queen?

According to different dictionaries, a queen is a female sovereign or monarch; she's the wife of a king, a woman eminent in power or in rank. She is somebody who behaves in an imperious manner, having supremacy or eminence in a given domain.

You don't just wake up a morning and decide that you are a queen.

A queen must be *noble,* that is, having or showing qualities of high morals and character, such as courage, generosity, or honor.

She must be *ready to serve*—to help, to work for, and to be of use.

She must be *trustworthy,* somebody you can rely on.

She must *possess knowledge and understanding of the constitution, history, and diplomacy* of her kingdom.

She must *desire to reunite.*

She must be *inspiring*, somebody people can look up to not as being perfect but as a role model.

She must *be comforting,* coming from her tenderness.

She must be *virtuous* and beautiful.

Entomologically speaking, a queen is a reproductive female in a colony of ants or bees. Fertile and fully developed, her function is to lay eggs. In other words, she has the duty of being fruitful. We're talking here about maturity, productivity, and leadership.

This is the definition of a queen according to the world where we live, according to human wisdom and understanding. But what does the wisdom of God say about a queen?

2

The Lady in Proverbs 31

In Proverbs 31:10–31 (KJV), King Solomon describes a kingdom lady, a daughter of the king, a queen.

> Who can find a virtuous woman? For her price is far above rubies. The heart of her husband doth safely trust in her, so that he shall have no need of spoil. She will do him good and not evil all the days of her life. She seeketh wool, and flax, and worketh willingly with her hands. She is like the merchants' ships; she bringeth her food from afar …

Do you see how he starts? In the first sentence, he says, "Who can find a virtuous woman?"

We don't usually look for something that we already have. To my own understanding, to find something or someone means you've been searching for it or for one. In other words, to get back to what I said earlier, we were not born as virtuous women or as queens, but we become ones. He continues by saying, "her price is far above rubies."

Rubies are gemstones in the same order as diamonds, sapphires, emeralds, and amethysts, which are generally known for their value. Just so that we have an understanding or a clearer vision of what this means, a certain jewel called the sunrise ruby was sold for over $30 million. It is considered a high-quality ruby, which can be extremely rare. And that's the price of only one. In the verse it says "rubies." That's plural. Just imagine if someone had to pay your dowry for that price or just offer you a ring of that price. How would you feel?

Well, a virtuous woman is worth more than that. When we read down to verse 31, we see different characteristics that make her virtuous.

- Verse 11: She is trustworthy. She gives honor.
- Verse 12: She's kind.
- Verses 13, 14, 19, 22: She's hardworking.
- Verse 15: She's organized and caring.
- Verses 16 and 24: She is moneywise.
- Verse 17: She's strong.
- Verse 18: She's watchful.
- Verse 20: She's generous and charitable.
- Verse 21: She's proactive and optimistic.
- Verses 22, 28, 31: She is praiseworthy.
- Verses 26 and 27: She's wise and kind.
- Verse 29: She has an excellent spirit.
- Verse 30: Above all, she fears the Lord.

Does it sound like something we have read before?

Let's go a little bit deeper. Let's see some examples in the Bible.

Some Bible Examples

Let's look at some examples of "kingdom ladies" in the Bible.

Ruth

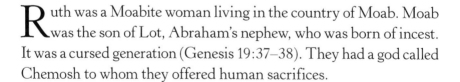

Ruth was a Moabite woman living in the country of Moab. Moab was the son of Lot, Abraham's nephew, who was born of incest. It was a cursed generation (Genesis 19:37–38). They had a god called Chemosh to whom they offered human sacrifices.

Ruth married Malhon, Naomi's son, an Israelite who took refuge in that land as they fled Bethlehem because of famine. She later accepted the God of the Israelites as her God and the Israelites as her own. Little did she know that was the beginning of a journey.

She lost her husband and decided to follow her mother-in-law. Ruth said,

> Where you go I will go, and you stay I will stay. Your people will be my people and your God my God. Where you die I will die and there will I be buried. (Ruth 1:16–17 KJV)

Even though Naomi had nothing left (she lost her husband and her two sons), she was born of a royal family. She understood that the Israelites and their God (the almighty King) were different people. She knew they were a chosen generation, a royal priesthood, a peculiar people (1 Peter 2:9), so she decided to know more about Him to serve Him and to work by the principles of His kingdom.

As Ruth embarked on that journey, she had many reasons to give up and go back to her people and live in obscurity. But she didn't allow her past, her mistakes, and her pains to hold her back in her process of becoming who the almighty King wanted her to be: a queen. She believed that there was still life to be lived, destinies to be fulfilled, and an ultimate reward to be with the almighty King at the end of these days. She moved forward in confidence.

Ruth showed respect and honor to her mother-in-law. She humbled herself and served her with love.

Remember, she left her own people (parents, friends, and family) to come to a land of people she didn't know. That's what I call separation.

We all know what separation is. Once again, Ruth didn't allow that to make her sit and wait for somebody else to provide food or other needs for her and her mother-in-law. It was in her hard work that she met the man God had prepared for her and brought her to the lineage of King David and the Messiah.

To put it in a few words, Ruth went through her process of becoming a queen. Life wasn't easy for her, contrary to the earthly system where a princess has everything brought to her on a platter of gold. She was born and raised in a wicked nation, she suffered the loss of her husband, and she went to live in a foreign land where she knew no one except Naomi. Though it may seem like all those things happened in a space of just few months, they actually took years.

I love the story of Ruth because I consider her a portrait of the noble womanhood—virtue, loyalty, peace, kindness, fear of the Lord, faithfulness, hardworking, diligence, obedience, and humility—which are kingdom values.

Esther

This is one of my favorites in the Bible. I connect with her story. Don't get me wrong; I was not captured by soldiers to be prepared as potential wife of a king, and I don't want to be. But I admire her courage and her character.

Esther (Hadassah of birth) was a Jewish woman of the tribe of Benjamin. She was raised in the Persian Empire by her elder cousin Mordecai after the death of her parents. Her ancestors were among the Jews who had been taken in captivity to Babylon. A time came when King Ahasuerus (the ruler at that time), on the advice of his counselors, decided to take a new wife. He sent his men to go and get all the beautiful young virgins of the land so that he could make his choice. Esther was among the ones brought to the palace, and this is where it starts to get interesting. Each young lady had to be presented before the king.

Now imagine a big country like what is described in Esther 1:1 (from India even to Ethiopia, over 127 provinces). How many young virgins do you think there were? I guess many.

> Before a young woman's turn came to go into King
> Xerxes, she had to complete twelve months of beauty
> treatments prescribed for the women, six months with
> oil of myrrh and six with perfumes and cosmetics.
> (Esther 2:12 NIV)

This passage always stokes my attention; they had to be prepared twelve months before they could see the king. Just to see him? I started asking myself some questions like, "What is the revelation behind this?" So I went on a journey to find the hidden meaning to this verse. I discovered that back in the day, the oil of myrrh was used for purification and healing. It was used for cleansing and restoration as well. (Just so we understand, the virgins were taken from all over the land, regardless of their social rankings.)

This process ensured a wholeness (we'll get deeper about this later) that started from the inside to reflect on the outside. The perfumes and cosmetics were obviously to enhance the appearance, to beautify, and to give a sweet fragrance.

The Bible says in Esther 2:15 (NIV),

> Now when the turn of Esther, the daughter of
> Abihail, the uncle of Mordecai, who had taken her
> for his daughter, was come to go in unto the King,
> she required nothing but what Hegai the King's
> chamberlain, the keeper of the women, appointed.
> And Esther obtained favor in the sight of all them that
> looked upon her.

I agree that Esther was beautiful. Esther 2:7 says, "And the maid was fair and beautiful." But do you think it's because of that outward beauty that she found favor in the sight of many? I don't think so. There were surely hundreds or maybe even thousands of young girls there, and do you think there was no other really beautiful girl among them?

There is a beauty that radiates from the inside to the outside. That's the kind of beauty that usually causes people to want to be around you and make you to find favor in the sight of many. Notice that all the other ladies had been given the opportunity to have whatever they desired to go and see the king. But when it was Esther's turn, by wisdom, she decided to take the king's chamberlain's advice. That's one part of it, but let's see other characteristics that made her a virtuous woman, a queen.

> So Esther's maid and her chamberlain's came and told it her. Then was the queen exceedingly grieved; and she sent raiment to clothe Mordecai and to take away his sackcloth from him: but he received it not. Then called Esther for Hatach, one of the King's chamberlains, whom he had appointed to attend upon her, and gave him a commandment to Mordecai, to know what it was, and why it was. (Esther 4:4–5 NIV)

Let's stop there for now.

- She hears that her father (cousin) is seated at the gate with his sackcloth; her first reflex is to send him raiment (that's caring).

- He refuses, yet she sends another chamberlain to enquire the reason for it (that's respect and humility). She could have said to herself, "After all, I am the queen now, I don't have time for that," or, "I already tried; he rejected my help." But she didn't.

> Then Mordecai commanded to answer Esther, Think not with thyself that thou shalt escape in the king's house, more than all the Jews. For if thou altogether holdest thy peace at this time, then shall there enlargement and deliverance arise to the Jews from another place; but thou and thy father's house shall be

destroyed: and who knoweth whether thou art come
to the kingdom for such a time as this? Then Esther
bade them return Mordecai this answer, Go, gather
together all the Jews that are present in Shushan,
and fast ye for me, and neither eat nor drink three
days, night or day: I also and my maidens will fast
likewise; and so will I go in unto the king, which is not
according to the law: and if I perish, I perish. (Esther
4:13–16 KJV)

In this passage, we see Queen Esther demonstrating courage and a
strong faith. It takes a woman who trusts in the Lord to make that
kind of decision. She was submissive but very confident. She had an
understanding of the kingdom constitution, of how to call on the
one who is King over all earthly kings. She knew that even though
she was a queen on this earth, she was first a queen in the heavenly
kingdom; it is the spiritual that controls the physical. So she called for
a fast, not only for her, but for all the Jews of the land and her maids
as well. That shows an understanding of who she was, her authority,
and walking in it.

I personally admire her firm assurance in the Lord: "I perish I perish."
She was ready to die for the kingdom's sake. Does that remind you
of something? Jesus said in John 15:13 (KJV), "Greater love hath no
man than this, that a man lay down his life for his friends."

On the third day of the fast, Esther put on her royal
robes and entered the inner court of the palace, just
across from the king's hall. The king was sitting on
his royal throne, facing the entrance. When he saw
Queen Esther standing there in the inner court, he
welcomed her and held out the gold scepter to her. So
Esther approached and touched the end of the scepter.
Then the king asked her, "What do you want, Queen

Esther? What is your request? I will give it to you, even if it is half the kingdom!"

And Esther replied, "If it please the king, let the king and Haman come today to a banquet I have prepared for the king. The king turned to his attendants and said, "Tell Haman to come quickly to a banquet, as Esther has requested." So the king and Haman went to Esther's banquet. And while they were drinking wine, the king said to Esther, "Now tell me what you really want. What is your request? I will give it to you, even if it is half the kingdom!" Esther replied, "This is my request and deepest wish. If I have found favor with the king, and if it pleases the king to grant my request and do what I ask, please come with Haman tomorrow to the banquet I will prepare for you. Then I will explain what this is all about." (Esther 5:1–8 NLT)

I love the way she knew chose her words with great wisdom. Compared to Vashti, the prior queen, who obtained favor in the sight of the king but misused it, Esther was conscious of it but still approached him with honor and wisdom. In the verse we just read, it is written that Esther again obtained favor in the sight of the king, who stood to hold out to her the golden scepter, knowing what the law said in such a case. And that's even before she opened her mouth to speak. The King of kings was by her side. To me, it sounds like a romantic drama.

As if it was not already awesome what he did, King Ahasuerus said, "What do you want, Queen Esther? What is your request? I will give it to you, even if it is half the kingdom!"

Hello, am I dreaming?

First of all, it was against the law to show up before the king without him inviting you—even as the queen—lest you be put to death. But then he is ready to give her half of his great kingdom? Do we get something?

Not only was she wise but she proved her objectivity and uprightness. How? The scriptures tells us that Haman was the most powerful official in the empire (Esther 3:1), but she didn't tremble before him. She knew what her mission was and that justice had to be done.

She brought the "battle" in her own place of comfort. Notice that when she said what she had to say to the king, he could have still decided not to believe her, but a greater King was operating on her behalf.

Esther had what it takes to be a queen. She was a virtuous woman who feared the Lord, and because she was a daughter of the King of kings, His scent and favor were on her. She was not self-ambitious in what she did but gracious and meek. Her story set a little picture of what the Messiah was going to do years after.

The next chapter, "One Night with the King," was actually from this story and its movie. I imagined what I would have done if I was given a chance to stand before the King of kings. It's more poetry, but I also consider it worship, worship here being defined as that time of intimacy with the King.

4

One Night with the King

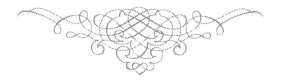

Imagine that, like Queen Esther, you were given the opportunity to have one night with the King. What would you do?

Let me tell you a little bit about myself.

I'm a lover. Everything that is poem, romance, arts, and nature I love. In getting to know Jesus, I've learned to fall in love with Him. It may sound crazy for some people, but yeah, it's possible.

You know when a girl falls in love with a guy, she wants to spend time with him, talk to him, walk with him. She wants to go to an intimate place where it will be just the two of them. They'll share a romantic night together, maybe with poems, love songs, and kisses or hugs. I know you know what I'm talking about.

Well, I like to do it with Him. I go on dates with Him. He's my King, my first lover. I talk to him about every single thing, just like with a confidant or a best friend. I love to sing Him songs and write Him poems, I share love words with Him.

In this part of the book, I want to give you a sample of one night with the King.

Lady: *To My Lover*

My beloved,
I believe words cannot express how I feel about You,
and there are just no words to praise You.
My lover, my friend, my Lord, my King,
I would like to share these words with You
Since my tender age I've known You.
I played with You, I laughed with You, I danced with You.
But then I didn't know how much You loved me.
I grew up, and You became an acquaintance to me.
Only once in a while I would say, "Hi," to you.
And then, silence.
I traveled far away from You.
I deliberately chose to play, laugh, and dance with other friends.
Somehow I knew You were looking at me, but I decided to ignore You.
You've watched me going through all my mess.
You called me, but I never bothered to answer.
I shut down every means of communication so that You couldn't call me.
Yet You still found a way to reach me.
After some tears and broken hearts, You were still there, waiting patiently for me to give it a try,
To let You love me.
And then You took time with me,
Despite my crises, fears, and excuses.
You proposed to me in a very funny way.

But saying yes was so far, but will still be the best decision I ever made in my life.

Since then, You took care of me.

You broke down the walls of my fears.

You brought out the best in me.

You made sure to count all my tears.

You showed so much patience with me.

You showered me with Your love.

You taught me,

You protected me,

You fought for me.

You delivered me from my mess.

You defend my cause all the time.

You keep on doing it, and You promise to always be there for me. Selah.

I said, "I do," on July 20 before many witnesses.

It was for better for worse.

But the worse can only come from me because you always give good.

I have tasted of the sweetest of love, Your love.

From now to the end of my days on this earth,

I give You my life, my soul, my body, my heart, and my mind.

I will love You and stay faithful to You,

Submit to You as the virtuous wife You made me to be.

If I fall, please help me.

I want to be with You at the Lamb's supper, dancing and singing to You, my King.

As it is written: "But he that is joined unto the Lord is one spirit,"

I will be one with You, learning at Your feet.

O that You may give me a heart that's just like Yours Because a love like Yours can never pass away but instead grows stronger every day.

To close this letter, I will say with a joyful and grateful heart,
My husband, my adorable Father,
My King, I love You.
May Your name be glorified in heaven, on earth, underneath the earth, and in our lives.

Your Princess

The King

I have loved thee with an everlasting love: therefore with loving-kindness have I drawn thee. (Jeremiah 31:3b KJV)

For I the Lord (your King) hath called thee as a woman forsaken and grieved in spirit, and a wife of youth, when thou wast refused, saith thy God. (Isaiah 54:6 KJV)

You are my witness, and my beloved whom I have chosen, so that you may know and believe me and understand that I am he. Before me no god was formed, nor will there be one after me. (Isaiah 43:10 NIV)

Others were given in exchange for you. I traded their lives for yours because you are precious to me. You are honored, and I love you. (Isaiah 43:4 NLT)

Behold, I have graven thee upon the palms of my hands; thy walls are continually before Me. (Isaiah 49:16 KJV)

I will contend with him that contendeth with thee. (Isaiah 49:25b KJV)

And when you'll be afraid remember: I the Lord (your King) will hold thy right hand, saying unto thee; fear not, I will help thee. (Isaiah 41:13 KJV)

For I know the thoughts that I think toward you … thoughts of peace and not of evil to give you an expected end. (Jeremiah 29:11 KJV)

So is my word that goes out from my mouth: It will not return to me empty, but will accomplish what I desire and achieve the purpose for which I sent it. (Isaiah 55:11 NIV)

I am the Lord, the God of all mankind. Is anything too hard for me? (Jeremiah 32:27 NIV)

Who kept the sea inside its boundaries as it burst from the womb and as I clothed it with clouds and wrapped it in thick darkness? (Job 38:8–9 NLT)

I am with you always [remaining with you perpetually—regardless of circumstance, and on every occasion], even to the end of the age. (Matthew 28:20b AMP)

Lady

O tell me, my heart,
What kind of love is this?
Speechless.
You are
More than enough,
More than a friend,
Bigger than every mountain.
Heaven and earth You've given me

You've lifted me.
I am
More than a conqueror,
More than victorious,
Beautiful in Your eyes,
Molded by Your love,
Amazed by Your greatness,
Speechless.
Tell me, my lips,
Whom shall I sing to?
My eyes,
Who are you longing to see?
Jesus is all I have.
My love,
The bread of my life,
My sweet wine,
My light,
My life,
My King.
This is a love letter to the best of lovers,
My husband, my friend,
My father, my King.
The sun shall pass,
The moon shall pass,
But His love will never stop shining for me.

The King

When no one looked on you with pity nor had
compassion enough to do any of these things for you;
they rather rejected you; even on the day you were
born you were despised by some, I saw it.

Then I passed by and saw you kicking about in your blood, (in your mess), and as you lay there in your blood I said to you, "Live!" I made you grow like a plant of the field. You grew and developed and entered puberty. Your breasts had formed and your hair had grown, yet you were stark naked.

Later I passed by, and when I looked at you and saw that you were old enough for love, I spread the corner of my garment over you and covered your naked body. I gave you my solemn oath and entered into a covenant with you … and you became mine.

I bathed you with water and washed the blood from you and put ointments on you. I clothed you with an embroidered dress and put sandals of fine leather on you. I dressed you in fine linen and covered you with costly garments. I adorned you with jewelry: I put bracelets on your arms and a necklace around your neck, and I put a ring on your nose, earrings on your ears and a beautiful crown on your head. So you were adorned with gold and silver; your clothes were of fine linen and costly fabric and embroidered cloth. Your food was honey, olive oil and the finest flour. You became very beautiful and rose to be a queen. I will make your fame spread among the nations on account of your beauty, because the splendor I am giving you is making your beauty perfect, declares the Sovereign Lord. (Ezekiel 16:5–14 NIV modified)

Lady

Sweet, sweet, sweet
Is the melody that You put in my heart.

In my eyes, tears.
In my ears, Your voice.
In my soul, peace.
In my mouth, praises.

The King

Fear not, for I have redeemed you;
I have called you by your name;
You are Mine. (Isaiah 43:1b ESV)

5

Love as the Identity of a Queen

> Love suffers long and is kind; love does not envy; love does not parade itself, is not puffed up; does not behave rudely, does not seek its own, is not provoked, thinks no evil; does not rejoice in iniquity, but rejoices in the truth; bears all things, believes all things, hopes all things, endures all things.
>
> 1 Corinthians 13:4–7 NKJV

In the process of becoming a queen, love is a must, as well as understanding it—even though we can't really fully understand this love we're talking about. If I may say, all the things we go through—persecution, rejection, suffering, and so on—work together to make us understand love and to teach us the agape love. There is *no* way you'll become a queen if you don't have love. In this kingdom where we come from, love is our identity: "Dear friends let us continue to love one another, for love comes from God. Anyone who loves is a child of God and knows God. But anyone who doesn't love doesn't know God, for God is love" (1 John 4:7–8 NLT).

We understand that to be a candidate for a presidential election, the first thing you need is citizenship. If you are not a citizen (you are just a permanent resident or a refugee), you don't have to think about it. Well, it's the same way it works in our kingdom. To become a queen, you first need to be a child of God. We're not talking about love as the world describes it. This is agape love, love as defined in 1 Corinthians 13:4–7, a selfless love.

What Is Love Then?

You can never hear 1 Corinthians 13:4–7 enough. It is one of the fundamental and key articles in our constitution.

In our kingdom, the two greatest laws are these:

> You must love the Lord your God with all your heart, all your soul, all your mind and all your strength and the second is to love your neighbor as yourself. No other commandment is greater than these. (Mark 12:30–31 NLT)

So it's all about love as having the following characteristics.

1. Love is Patient

Being patient means being able to bear or tolerate what seems unbearable—such as delays, problems, or suffering—without becoming angry or frustrated. According to *Merriam-Webster's Dictionary*, it means bearing pains or trials calmly or without complaint; manifesting forbearance under provocation or stain, steadfast despite opposition, difficulty, or adversity. Another version says, "to quietly and steadily persevere."

In some other versions of the Bible, it says, "love suffers long." You can't say you love if you can't endure suffering. Sounds harsh, right? But it's the truth. It's the first adjective used to describe love, so it's the first thing you need when we talk about love.

Love requires us to be slow to anger and to learn how to endure personal wrongs without retaliating, or in other words, to repay evil with good. It demands that we should create room for others' faults without coming down on them; that is forbearance. No matter the persecution, trials, adversities, or storms, you stay confident, waiting on the King's time of fulfilling His Word with all submission.

> And so, after Abraham had patiently endured, he obtained the promise. (Hebrews 6:15 KJV)

Do you see this? And Abraham was called the friend of God (James 2:23). Yet he also had to be patient and go through trials before he could obtain the promise.

In this process, we're constantly going to be under the reproaches of men through trials and persecution. Nevertheless, for the sake of our heavenly King and for our kingdom, and in imitation of Him, we'll need to be merciful just as He is, not hasty to pay back or quick to resent. We must exercise forbearance and tolerance.

2. Love is Kind (Merciful)

To be kind is to be generous, helpful, and caring about other people. A kind person is compassionate and does not act out of his or her own interest. Kindness, according to the kingdom, means to show care, mercy, and compassion even in response to harsh treatment.

> Do to others as you would have them do to you. If you love those who love you, what credit is that to you? Even sinners love those who love them. And if you do

good to those who are good to you, what credit is that
to you? Even sinners do that … But love your enemies,
do good to them, and lend to them without expecting
to get anything back. Then your reward will be great,
and you will be children of the Most High, because
he is kind to the ungrateful and wicked. Be merciful,
just as your Father is merciful. (Luke 6:27–31 NIV)

This is not easy to do, but it's possible with Jesus. He doesn't give us
more than what we can bear nor teach us what is impossible to do. If
we look at it with human eyes, then there's no way we can. This mercy
is to yield to the tempers and humors of others and to accommodate
yourself to others' infirmities, manners, and weaknesses in all
wisdom and discernment.

3. Love Does Not Envy

Envy is when you long or desire to have or possess something that
someone else has. It's also what the Bible calls "covetousness." It
generally comes out of a feeling of comparison. It causes rivalry and
competition, which are against Christian values. According to the
kingdom's constitution, we complete each other; we don't compete.

So that there should be no division in the body, but
that its parts should have equal concern for each other.
(1 Corinthians 12:25 NIV)

We are all one body, and each one of us is a part of it (1 Corinthians
12:27 NIV). The eye cannot say to the hand, "I don't need you!" And
the head cannot say to the feet, "I don't need you" (1 Corinthians
12:21 NIV).

Imagine that you wake up one Monday morning, and your eyes want
to act or behave like your hands. Or your hands want to be on the

ground, while your feet are thinking. It sounds awkward, right? I agree because all parts of our bodies are supposed to work together. There is no part that is better than the other: "on the contrary, those parts of the body that seem to be weaker are indispensable" (1 Corinthians 12:22 NIV), simply because every single part has a role to play.

There's no need for envy among children of the kingdom. Envy comes out of a heart of greed and selfishness. If you love someone, you want to help the person, and if the person has more than what you have, it's okay because we all have the same Father, who is not partial and shows no favoritism. James 4:2–3 (NLT) says, "you want what you don't have, so you scheme and kill to get it. You are jealous of what others have, but you can't get it, so you fight and wage war to take it away from them. Yet you don't have what you want because you don't ask God for it. And even when you ask, you don't get it because your motives are all wrong—you want only what will give you pleasure."

Our Father, the almighty King, has a plan for everyone who is called his child.

> Then peter replied "I see clearly that God shows no favoritism. In every nation, He accepts those who fear Him and do what is right." (Acts 10:34–35 NIV)

When we read these, we see that envying someone or something is a waste of time and a lack of understanding of what this love is all about. It is also in prayer that we can fight this feeling because after all, we are still flesh and blood, and the flesh is always at war with the spirit.

4. Love vaunteth not itself

To vaunt is to brag about something. *Merriam-Webster's Dictionary* says, "it's to make a vain display of one's own worth or attainments."

Some of us like to remind others what we did for them or what we've achieved. I've often seen it in relationships. Let's say the Lord decided to bless Mary, and she did many good things for Pascal, such as helping him to get a good job, leading him to the Lord. and giving him a car. The day Pascal does something that Mary doesn't like and she feels offended, the tendency is that she'll start reminding him of everything she did for him or even go about telling people how much she did for him and how he's being ungrateful.

Bragging comes out of a heart of pride.

> This is what the Lord says: let not the wise boast of their wisdom or the strong boast of their strength or the rich boast of their riches, but let the one who boasts boast about this: that they have the understanding to know me, that I am the Lord, who exercises kindness, justice and righteousness on earth, for in these I delight. (Jeremiah 9:23–24 NIV)

Nothing that we have is ours; it's just because of His mercy.

5. Love Is Not Puffed Up

When you're puffed up, you feel self-important, arrogant. In fact, you are very proud of yourself. Romans 12:3, 16 (NIV) says,

> For by the grace given to me, I say to every one of you: do not think of yourself more highly than you ought, but rather think of yourself with sober judgment, in accordance with the faith God has distributed to each of you … lie in harmony with one another. Do not be proud, but be willing to associate with people of low position. Do not be conceited.

We are nothing if it's not by Christ. There is nothing that we do to deserve life. There's neither theory nor arithmetical formula that we can apply to keep us alive, give us what we have, or assure us that what we have today is permanent. No one is indispensable.

An example of someone who was puffed up in the Bible is King Nebuchadnezzar. The Lord lifted him to a very high position; he had sovereignty, greatness, glory, and splendor. Then he started to feel self-important. He said, "Is not this the great Babylon I have built as the royal residence, by my mighty power and the glory of my majesty?" (Daniel 4:28–30 NIV).

Pride came in, and the Bible says, "When his heart became arrogant and hardened with pride, he was deposed from his royal throne and stripped of his glory" (Daniel 5:20 NIV).

Because love is our identity in our kingdom, pride is definitely the last thing we want to cherish because, "Pride goeth before destruction and a haughty spirit before a fall" (Proverbs 16:18 KJV).

6. Love Does Not Behave Unseemly/ Doesn't Dishonor Others

Another version says, "is not rude." There are people who, because they hold a certain position that gives them authority, can be very rude. Some are just rude by nature or have become so because of experiences.

To behave unseemly is to behave in an inappropriate manner, to be indiscreet, indelicate, ungentlemanly or unladylike, to be indecent.

To be rude is to be impolite, especially in a deliberate way, to be rough in manners or behavior.

Royalty comes with character. To become a king in this world or when you are born into a royal family, they make sure you are taught politeness and good behavior; they teach you how to be courteous. Matthew 5:16 (ERV) says, "In the same way, you should be a light for other people. Live so that they will see the good things you do and praise your Father in heaven."

We are called to represent our King, the King of kings: "Since God chose us to be the holy people he loves, we must clothe ourselves with tenderhearted mercy, kindness, gentleness and patience" (Colossians 3:12 NIV).

> Work at living in peace with everyone, and work at living a holy life, for those who are not holy will not see the Lord. Look after each other so that none of you fails to receive the grace of God. Watch out that no poisonous root of bitterness grows up to trouble you, corrupting many. (Hebrews 12:14–15 NLT)

A daughter of the kingdom should not behave unseemly or be rude to others. When it does happen, it's generally coming from roots that we have allowed to grow inside us. It can be bitterness, jealousy, envy, stress, or resentment. So check the roots.

We should learn how to keep our composure in all situations and to overlook offenses. It is important to think about others and how they will feel. Doesn't the second-greatest commandment say to "Love our neighbors as ourselves"? (Galatians 5:14). We can't be rude to ourselves, and we know how we feel when someone is rude to us. So why do it to others?

> Do to others whatever you would like them to do to you. This is the essence of all that is taught in the law and the prophets. (Matthew 7:12 NLT)

Love does no wrong to others, so love fulfills the requirements of God's law. (Romans 13:10 NLT)

7. Love Seeketh Not Her Own

Agape love is self-sacrificing; it doesn't demand its rights. It's all about selflessness. It cares more for others. It's not, "Me first and then the others." We saw the example of Queen Esther, who was ready to die for her people. The ultimate and greatest example is our Lord Jesus, who died on the cross so that we might have eternal life. He left His throne and all its treasures in heaven to come down on earth, where He was persecuted and rejected. The Bible says,

> He was pierced for our transgressions, he was bruised for our iniquities; the punishment that brought us peace was on Him, and by his wounds we are healed. (Isaiah 53:11 NIV)

He did nothing wrong, but He died so that you and I can have peace. He didn't have to, but because of love, He sacrificed Himself.

> He is the radiance of the glory of God and the exact imprint of his nature, and he upholds the universe by the word of his power. (Hebrews 1:3 ESV)

Did He owe us anything? No! He seeketh not his own, and that is why we are still alive. Once we receive Christ and believe in His name, He puts in us the ability to love others just as He loves us. But we cannot give more than what we have. That is why we first need to fill up our love tank by receiving God's love before we can share it with others. It is the level of intimacy that we have with Christ that will determine how well we will be able to love others. God is Love.

> You must have the same attitude that Christ Jesus had. Though he was God, he did not think of equality

with God as something to cling to. Instead, he gave up his divine privileges; he took the humble position of a slave and was born as a human being. When he appeared in human form, he humbled himself in obedience to God and died a criminal's death on a cross. Therefore, God elevated him to the place of highest honor and gave him the name above all other names. (Philippians 2:5–9 NLT)

8. Love Is Not Easily Provoked (Easily Angered)

True love is not touchy. Some of us are so easily offended that people around us have to behave like they are walking on eggs. We are bad-tempered and get angry easily.

Understand this, my dear brothers and sisters: You must all be quick to listen, slow to speak, and slow to get angry. Human anger does not produce the righteousness God desires. (James 1:19–20 NLT)

To be easily provoked is to get easily angry. You feel offended by something, and you desire to fight back. The Bible recommends us to be slow to anger because the anger of man doesn't achieve God's righteousness.

Wisdom says,

Short-tempered people do foolish things, and schemers are hated; you should control your temper, for anger labels you a fool and only fools vent their anger, but the wise quietly hold it back; A hot-tempered person starts fights; but a cool-tempered person stops them; it is better to be patient than powerful and it is even much better to have self-control than to conquer a city. (Proverbs 14:17; Ecclesiastes 7:9; Proverbs 29:11; 15:18; 16:32 NLT)

Ouch! This one pierced me like an arrow because I know what it is to be easily provoked or easily angered. By nature, I'm a joyful person, but I used to be so easily angered, and I can tell you it's a daily process. But then I learned in psychology that anger is a secondary feeling, meaning there's a primary feeling—guilt, trauma, inferiority complex, ego, fear, and so on—that leads to anger itself. Most of the time it's because the ego was touched. And who says ego says pride, self, or flesh. So now, every time I want to get angry I ask myself, "What is actually behind my anger? Is it an inferiority complex, or is it guilt? Why am I angry?"

If you're honest with yourself, you'll recognize where the issue is really coming from, then you can ask the Lord to help you. Getting angry is not a sin but is what we do when we are angry, and that creates a problem. But as a woman called into royalty, self-control and patience have to be our daily shower.

9. Love Doesn't Keep Record/Score of the Sins of Others (Forgiveness)

When people hurt us, we try to find a place in our hearts to forgive and let go. But then it happens again and again and again. It becomes hard to let go, and we ask, "how long shall I continue to take it?" What happened? We kept record. God, in His all-sufficiency and greatness, shows us an example: "I, even I, am He who blots out your transgressions for my own sake; and I will not remember your sins" (Isaiah 43:25 NKJV).

If the Lord had to remind us of all the times we sinned against Him, the feeling of guilt that would come upon us would be too heavy to bear. Peter asked Jesus,

"Lord how many times shall I forgive my brother who sins against me? Up to seven times?" And Jesus answered "I tell you, not seven times, but seventy-seven times." (Matthew 18:21–22 NIV)

And this is daily. In other words, we should not count it. Just forgive and let go.

Matthew 6:14–15 (NIV) says it like this:

For if you forgive other people when they sin against you, your heavenly Father will also forgive you. But if you do not forgive others their sins, your Father will not forgive your sins.

You can also read Mark 11:25 (NIV).

We know that we all have sin, and if we say we don't, then we make God a liar. There is not a day we'll not sin. Yet we always want Him to forgive us anytime we come to Him in repentance.

Imagine that one night you kneel by your bed and ask God to forgive you for the sin that you keep on telling yourself you'll not do again. And He answers you, "This is not the first time. How long shall I continue to take it?"

I don't know about you, but as for me, I will roll on the floor, start a funeral service, and cry like I never did until He says that He has forgiven me.

Colossians 3:13 (NIV) says, "Bear with each other and forgive one another; if any of you has a grievance against someone, forgive as the Lord forgave (and keep on forgiving) you." He forgives us so that we forgive others. Forgiveness, according to our kingdom, requires that we do not calculate every time someone hurts us. Grace has been given to us for that. I understand that this is easier said than done, but it is possible. I'll talk more about it later in this book.

10. Love Doesn't Rejoice about Injustice (or Wrongdoing), but Rejoices When Truth Wins Out

> O people of Israel do not rejoice as other nations do. For you have been unfaithful to your God, hiring yourselves out like prostitutes, worshipping other gods on every threshing floor. (Hosea 9:1 NLT)

The book of Hosea talks about how the children of Israel abandoned God to worship other gods (Baal, Asherah, a Canaanite storm god and fertility god). They were feasting with other sinners. They were children of the King, but they took part in idol worship as other nations did, even though they knew the law said,

> You shall not make for yourself an image in the form of anything in heaven above or on the earth beneath or in the waters below. You shall not bow down to them or worship them; for I, the Lord your God, am a jealous God, punishing the children for the sin of the parents to the third and fourth generation of those who hate me, but showing love to a thousand generations of those who love me and keep my commandments. (Exodus 20:4–6 NIV)

They lived as if they were not God's people, feasting and rejoicing in their evildoing.

When you love someone, you don't take pleasure in doing things that you know will hurt that person.

I like to compare idolatry to adultery. They are almost the same. For me, idolatry is adultery toward God. When we put something before Him, or have another god we worship, we are cheating on Him. That's why in the book of Hosea, God asked His servant to take a prostitute as a wife because He wanted to illustrate, in a metaphorical way, the relationship He had with Israel, which applies to us today as well.

Now idolatry was used in this case as an example of iniquity. The basic idea of this is not to take pleasure in doing things that are evil in His sight; it grieves Him. Instead, rejoice in everything that is truth.

> hold on to what is good, reject every kind of evil. (1 Thessalonians 5:21–22 NIV)

Not to rejoice in wrongdoing is also not to rejoice when somebody falls into sin. It doesn't matter if it is a friend, a brother, someone you don't like, or an enemy.

> Do not rejoice when your enemies fall, don't be happy when they stumble for the Lord will be displeased with you and will turn His anger away from them. (Proverbs 24:17–18 NLT)

In the book of Jonah, we see an example. The Lord told Jonah to go and tell the people of Nineveh to repent from their sins and to turn back to him. But Jonah refused because he knew that God is a merciful and compassionate God, slow to get angry, and He was ready to turn back from destroying them. And effectively, God had mercy on them, so Jonah got angry. He wanted to see them destroyed because he remembered all the pain the people caused them. But we are to be merciful just as our Father is. For it's His heartbeat that none should perish but for all to be saved, to know the truth, and to be set free. When only one soul is out of darkness, there's great joy in heaven.

11. Love Bears All Things (Never Gives Up)/Puts Up with Anything

Have you ever felt like, "Father, I thank You that You never gave up on me, even when I was taking pleasure in the evil things of this world, when people ran away from me, or when they gave up on me because of my nasty attitude"? I do. Sometimes when I look in my past, I'm like, "If You'd abandoned me in that mess, I'd be dead by now."

How many times have we given up on somebody or on God because of what we see or what we think we can't bear? For love's sake, Jesus bore on Him a chastisement that was supposed to be ours, death on the cross.

To give up is defined as ceasing to make an effort, to resign oneself to failure. To bear is to carry, to support the weight of, to sustain. In other words, when we say we love, we are supposed to bear the weight that comes with persecutions, trials, challenges, and storms of this life without ceasing to fight and resign to failure. In our kingdom, the battles are real.

> we wrestle not against flesh and blood. (Ephesians 6:10 KJV)

> the weapons of our warfare are not carnal. (2 Corinthians 10:4 KJV)

We are in a real warfare, but we are not fighting each other. The enemy—the devil—attacks our relationship with each other and our relationship with God a lot.

If Jesus had given up the moment He was wounded, we would not have salvation today.

Bear with each other and forgive one another if any of you has a grievance against someone. Forgive as the Lord forgave you. (Colossians 3:13 NIV)

12. Love Believes All Things (Trust God Always)

I like the NLT version that says, "never loses faith." Some people might use this passage to spiritually blackmail you. What do I mean? You know when somebody uses scriptures to get what he or she wants from you, like, "If you really love me, you'll believe everything I tell you. Doesn't the Bible say love believes all things?"

Error! Error! Error! Love doesn't mean you should be stupid.

Here it's talking about believing in God, believe that what He says He will do; He will surely do it. It doesn't also mean you shouldn't believe what people are telling you. When it comes to individuals, it's a good thing to ask for the spirit of discernment because we shouldn't be carried by any kind of doctrine or eloquent speeches. We should always try it to see if it's truth or deception.

What is faith? "Now faith is the substance of things hoped for, the evidence of things not seen" (Hebrews 11:1 KJV). Another version says, "It's the confidence in what we hope for and the assurance about what we do not see."

> Faith is the response of our spirit to the word of God
> and not of our mind, even when it sounds impossible.
> (Apostle Efon Brillant)

The eleventh chapter of the book of Hebrews lists a number of people who had faith and how they were rewarded because they believed. Never lose faith, no matter what happens.

> Faith comes by hearing, hearing by the word of God. (Romans 10:17 KJV)

That is, as long as you expose yourself to the Word of God—reading the Bible, meditating on the Word, listening to good sermons, going to church, and so on—your faith will stand strong and grow. When it comes to human beings, it is good to give time to see if the person is worth our trust. Time will reveal the person's nature, and by discernment and wisdom, we will know if we should believe or not, for the heart of Man is desperately wicked. However, even the most honest person, worth our trust, can disappoint us at a certain point. Should we give up on that person or tag him as a betrayer? That is something to give a second thought because we should still keep in mind that we have an adversary the devil who is always ready to destroy our relationships, especially the ones that are important for the fulfillment of our destinies. The amplified version puts it this way: "Love looks for the best in each one". What a word?

13. Love Hopes in All Things (Remains Steadfast During Difficult Times)

> The Lord delights in those who fear him, who put their hope in his unfailing love. (Psalm 147:11 NIV)

To hope is to desire with expectation and confidence the fulfillment of something you long for. To go deeper, the apostle Paul said that "hope that is seen is not; we hope for what we do not see." (Romans 8: 24-25)

Hope and faith are much related to each other. There's no faith without hope and no hope without faith.

As we saw before, faith is the confidence of things hoped for. For your faith to stay alive, you need hope, which is defined as the anchor of our souls in Hebrews 6:19. In other words, our souls need hope to stand still, as we see in Proverbs 13:12 (NIV):

> Hope deferred (postponed or delayed) makes the heart sick, but a longing (a desire) fulfilled is a tree of life.

The main reason a ship needs an anchor is to ride out storms so that it is not blown off course or into the rocks of reefs nearby. Even when there is no storm, a ship still needs an anchor so that it will not drift and maybe hit something and then sink. It's the same for our souls. When the storms of life arise, or even during the quiet seasons of life, if our souls don't have an anchor, which is hope, we might hit something ahead and then sink.

14. Love Endures All Things (Through Every Circumstance)

The Message Bible version says, "love keeps going to the end." In other versions, Luke 21:19 appears as,

> By your endurance you will gain your lives. (ESV)

> By your [patient] endurance [empowered by the Holy Spirit] you will gain your souls. (AMP)

When I was in high school, I was very good at running the 100 meters or 200 meters. I loved it. In ten to twenty seconds, you're done. But when it came to the 800 meters or 1,500 meters, forget it; I didn't like it. Sometimes I would run and feel like my lungs would fall into my stomach. Then at one point, I decided to faint so that they would not ask me to continue. I couldn't endure. And you know what? Some people followed me and did the same thing. Oh, God, it was funny.

That's what we see in this generation nowadays; we don't want to endure things that come our way. We want to do it in ten to twenty seconds, like the 200 meter race and we're done.

But this race that we're in demands endurance. And if we say we love Him, then we'll endure all the trials and persecutions till the end because we want to see and be with Him. It makes us perfect.

> Count it all joy, my brothers, when you meet trials of various kinds, for you know that the testing of your faith produces steadfastness. And let steadfastness have its full effect, that you may be perfect and complete, lacking in nothing. (James 1:2–4 ESV)

And when it comes to our fellows, we'll endure their bad tempers, brokenness, attitudes, sins, mistakes, and weaknesses. One important thing that I want us to notice is, like I said, when I decided to faint, many followed me and started doing the same thing. Those who were tired but so determined to go till the end followed except the one who was ahead and finished the race. In Luke 21:19, which we read earlier, says that by patient endurance, we will gain our souls. Not just our souls but also the souls of those who are following us, imitating us, or looking up to us.

Apostle Paul said in 2 Timothy 4:7 (ESV), "I have fought the good fight, I have finished the race, I have kept the faith." And Hebrews 10:36 (ESV) tells us, "For you have need of endurance, so that when you have done the will of God, you may receive the promise."

In a few words, love is about professing it and about acting it out. If we can grasp just a little bit of what this agape love is really about, then we'll be transformed in the way we see and do things. I pray that as we read the Word of God, the eyes of our understanding will be enlightened, and we'll be able to see like Him and to love like Him.

> When I think of all this, I fall to my knees and pray to the Father, the King, the Creator of everything in heaven and on earth. I pray that from his glorious, unlimited resources, He will empower us with inner

strength through his spirit; then Christ will make His home in our hearts as we trust in Him. Our roots will grow down into God's love and keep us strong. May we all have the power to understand, (as all queens of this kingdom should), how wide, how long, how high and how deep this love is. May we experience the love of Christ, though it is too great to fully understand, so that we'll be made complete with all fullness of life and power that comes from God. (Ephesians 3:14–19 NLT)

Love never fails.

6

A Love Story

His Love

Lord, have we really comprehended the breadth, the length, the depth, and the height of Your love? Have we known Your love? Do we have an understanding of that love? I look at Your works, the wonders You do, and I stand amazed. When I think about Your love, my God, I lose my breath. It is something I can't explain; my human brain cannot process it. It's so, so …

I fell in love before. I was crazily in love with this young guy. I loved him, and he loved me too. Or should I say I thought I knew what love was. In that love there was pride, arrogance, abusive words, pains, fear of being rejected, and casting stones at each other.

I wrote songs, I wrote poems, I shed tears in that relationship. I also lost a part of my self-esteem in it. No matter the efforts, it didn't work. We broke up. After that I went on, again in a wrong relationship, that destroyed me emotionally. I thought I was losing my mind, that I wasn't good enough to keep a relationship. I lost my trust, my confidence. I became so bitter, so broken inside. I'd been loved the wrong way, and I also loved the wrong way. It destroyed my inner man. I got pain in my soul. Then He came and showed me true love, real love, agape love—the perfect love.

He taught me how to fall in love for real; falling in love with Him. A love that is patient and kind, not envious, not boastful, not proud, not rude. A love that doesn't demand its own way. It's not irritable and doesn't keep a record of being wronged. A love that never gives up.

He took me out of my mess—a broken heart, bitterness, resentment, unforgiveness, impatience, filthiness, malice, wrath, jealousy, foolishness, immorality, low self-esteem, rejection, prideful, and He said,

> Come. Come unto me, as you are, weary and burdened and I will give you rest. (Matthew 11:28 KJV)

> Come because nothing can separate you from my love; not tribulation, not distress, not persecution, not famine, not nakedness, not peril, not sword, Nothing! (Romans 8:35 KJV)

He said to me, "You are mine". He took time to cleanse me and wash me. When I fell and dirtied myself again, He still wanted me to come closer to Him. I got angry, I went against Him; He forgave me even before I opened my mouth to say sorry.

His anger lasts only a moment, but His favor lasts a lifetime; He said, "You may weep for the night, but I'll cause you to rejoice in the morning." (Psalms 30:5 KJV)

His love heals me; it makes me feel secure and strong. It delivers me and transforms me. I love Him because he loved me first (1 John 4:19). He wiped away my tears and taught me not to fear for His perfect love drives out all fears (1 John 4:18). Many times we profess to love someone, and at the first disappointment, we are ready to leave. But the love He showed me and that He is teaching me is a love that covers all wrongs (1 Peter 4:8).

I love what King Solomon said about love: "Many waters cannot quench love, nor rivers drown it. If a man tried to buy love with all his wealth, his offer would be utterly scorned" (Songs of Solomon 8:7 NIV).

He had a revelation of the kind of love my lover shares. I love that King, I seriously do. I am blessed to be loved by Him. I love Him with all my heart, with all my soul, with all my mind for this is the greatest commandment. This is what He has given me, so I'm writing Him songs, I'm writing Him poems, and I'm shedding tears. This time around, it's with joy in my heart and peace in my mind because He is worthy of it all. I didn't deserve this love, but He deserves all of me and all that I have. Falling in love with Him is the greatest thing I've ever done in my life.

This is my story with Him. You should have yours. Strive to fall in love with Jesus. His love is the only pill we need against rejection, depression, and other ills. We are busy looking for love outside, trying to make people love us, ready to change so that they can accept us, but no matter what we do, it's never enough. When you love Him, He is there for you, not asking you to do anything before He accepts you. You come as you are, and He does the rest. We struggle with rejection when the Almighty has already accepted us a long time ago.

Loving Again

When your heart has been broken one or many times, even though you've received God's love and healing, it's not automatic that you'll love again as if nothing ever happened. After I got saved and fell in love with the Lord, I was so passionate, and I wanted to do everything for God. Then I also remember telling Him, "Lord, I give You all of me, but please do not allow me to fall in love again. If I have to love again, it has to be my husband, that's it. If I experience heartbreak again, it will take me to my grave because it's so painful."

Oh my God! I'm still laughing as I'm writing it. Was I joking? No. I was very serious. I just wanted to love God and do His work until the right one came along. Do you think God listened to my prayer? Of course He did. But He surely didn't answer the way I was expecting Him to. Different men came to me to ask me out, and every time I brought it before God because I was conscious that He knew best, and our natural eyes can deceive us. Some were believers, some were not. At the end of the day, God will always give an answer. Sometimes it happened that I was considering one, but then God either used somebody to tell me or tell me personally, "No, wait on your husband." At this point, I was still on my guard that no one should enter my heart until this one came. Oh, Lord, he was a nice guy. He told me he was interested and that he wanted to know me better. We used to talk about ministry and spiritual life. He could be very encouraging. And before I could realize it, I started having an interest in him too. So as usual, I brought it before God and asked Him to show me who that guy truly was and if he was the one I was waiting for.

As time went by, I discovered he was married. You can imagine the level of disappointment. I won't say I was in love with him, but at that point, feelings were already involved. I was hurt because I was starting to think that he was the right one. That's why I said our natural senses can so deceive us. Then I went back to God and asked Him why. "Why did You allow it to happen? I thought we had an agreement that I will only feel that way again when it will be my husband." I was so upset. I seriously poured out my heart to God. And the Lord reminded me of a sermon I heard in which the man of God talked about how the things in or the areas of our lives that we do not totally surrender to God—or those things in our lives that we fear—are the very aspects that the enemy will use to bring us down. So we should just submit it all and trust God.

Was that really comforting? No. But at least I understood God's way. I could see the difference between pain without God and pain with God. No matter what, I could feel His love for me.

Did I get better? No way. Instead, I built walls around my heart. I made sure not to allow any man to speak to me in any way. I got as busy as I could. I was barely going out. My life was church, work, home. Though I desired to meet the Mr. Right, I was too afraid.

Ha, ha! I love God's sense of humor. I can imagine Him at that time, laughing as He watched me making arrangements on how not to fall again. Guess what? The next man who came into my life didn't have to go anywhere to see me. He saw my picture in one of my friends' phone and started inquiring about me, until he came to meet me in person. Now I know you'll be curious to know if that was Mr. Right, but I'll keep it for my next book, where I will talk about it in detail.

For now, I just want to point out that it was then that God started teaching me to love again. Surely I wouldn't forget my past experiences, but I would learn from them. I learned to see the difference between eros love and agape love.

The first thing that the Lord told me when this man came around was to take my walls down. I was so concerned and asked, "But, Lord, I'll feel so vulnerable. I'll feel naked. I don't want to get hurt again." And He said to me, "Your walls will not stop him, but they will stop Me from operating in your life. I need you to trust Me." Trust was the main thing that God required from me if wanted Him to teach me how to love again.

Because relationships are not the main theme of this book, I won't go into much detail. But He showed me so many practical things regarding this love we're talking about.

> Such love has no fear, because perfect love expels all fear. If we are afraid, it is for fear of punishment, and this shows that we have not fully experienced his perfect love. (1 John 4:18 NLT)

On the next few pages are the words of a woman who was freed from the pain of rejection, received His love, and learned to love again.

> Dilemma?
> Heaven or earth?
> Above or beneath?
> Spirit or body?
> Father or son?
> Divinity or humanity?
> Should my heart be torn in between?
> In fact, love or love?
> Him or him?
> Is there any choice to make?
> The first one loved me first.
> The second one loved me first too.
>
> I fell in love with both of them.
> One is perfect and loves me no matter my flaws.
> The other one is not perfect, but he loves me still.
> They both know how to put a smile on my face.
> One is always there wherever I go, always ready to contend with them who contend with me.
> The other one is not always there; in fact, he was not there when I really needed a shoulder to cry on.
> But they both care for me.
> Certainly one more than the other.

One calls me the apple of his eyes.
The other one calls me His beloved.
And they both want me to see a husband in them.
Is it hard to choose?
No.
There's no choice to make.
They are Father and son,
And like we usually say,
Like Father, like son.
One thing is sure.
The son can never love me as the Father will.
The Father loves the son;
The son loves me.
I love the Father;
The Father loves me.
I love the son;
The son loves the Father.
Amazing, no?
His Father is also my Father.
I am one with the Father and
One with the son.
The love of one is divine
The love of the other is humanly divine.
In brief, it's all about love.

7

Understanding the Constitution and History of Our Kingdom

What is a constitution?

A "constitution" is defined as the fundamental and basic rules governing the conduct of a nation or kingdom, and establishing its concept, character, and structure. It's usually a document, general in nature, and embodying the aspirations and values of it writers and subjects. It is also defined as a written instrument embodying the basic principles and laws of a nation/kingdom that determine the powers and duties of the government and guarantee certain rights to the people in it.

What is history? It's a chronological record of significant events, such as those affecting a nation or a kingdom, often including an explanation of their causes. In this part of the book I'd like us to see the importance of understanding the constitution of our kingdom. In the process of becoming a queen, it is very crucial and of great necessity.

First things first. You belong to this kingdom if you are born of God. You can be born as a princess, but a princess who knows nothing about her identity is worthless. It's only when you get to know the King and understand that He is your Father that you discover the princess in you.

> But to as many as did receive and welcome Him, He gave the right [the authority, the privilege] to become children of God, that is, to those who believe in (adhere to, trust in, and rely on) His name—who were born, not of blood [natural conception], nor of the will of the flesh [physical impulse], nor of the will of man [that of a natural father], but of God [that is, a divine and supernatural birth—they are born of God—spiritually transformed, renewed, sanctified]. (John 1:12–13 AMP)

Second, the One who rules this kingdom is the Creator of the entire universe: "For God is the King over all the earth. Praise him with a psalm. God reigns above the nations, sitting on his holy throne" (Psalm 47:7–8 NLT)

There is a kingdom:

> They shall speak of the glory of Your kingdom, and talk of Your power, to make known to the sons of men His mighty acts, and the glorious majesty of His kingdom. Your kingdom is an everlasting kingdom, and Your dominion endures throughout all generations. (Psalm 145:11–13 NKJV)

Now every kingdom, like every nation, has a constitution. There are laws and rules that you must follow, as well as rights that are given to the citizens of that nation/kingdom. And it has a history. The kingdom of God is not of this world. The principles that rule this kingdom can be the opposite of the principles that rule most of nations of this world. Our kingdom operates differently from the system of this world. We function by absolute monarchy, while this world functions by a form of democracy in most of the nations.

Monarchy is where a kingdom is headed by a king or a queen, while democracy is a government run by elected representatives. In a democracy, the people have the right to actively participate in politics, civic life, and decision-making. They elect the person they want to see as the head of the government. The rule of law limits the power of the government. Power is given to the citizens. It flows from the people to the leaders of government, and they can question its decisions. But in absolute monarchy, the one who rules is an autocrat. An autocracy is a system of government in which supreme power is concentrated in the hands of one person, whose decisions are subject to neither external legal restraints nor regularized mechanisms of popular control, and who has absolute power over the state and government. The problem that most of us have today is that because we are used to living under a democracy in this world, we want to apply the same system with God. But it doesn't work like that.

Can you imagine the clay telling the potter what he has to do or what he is supposed to do? "Family of Israel … you are like the clay in the potter's hands, and I am the potter" (Jeremiah 18:6 ERV).

The Bible says God created us in His image. He took the dust of the earth and formed us: "And the Lord God formed man of the dust of the ground, and breathed into his nostrils the breath of life; and man became a living being" (Genesis 2:7 NKJV).

So because God's kingdom is a monarchy,

> Are you going to object "so how can God blame us for anything since he's in charge of everything?" If the big decisions are already made, what say do we have in

it? Who in the world do you think you are to second-guess God? Do you for one moment suppose any of us knows enough to call God into question? Clay doesn't talk back to the fingers that mold it, saying, "Why did you shape me like this?" Isn't it obvious that a potter has a perfect right to shape one lump of clay into a vase for holding flowers and another into a pot for cooking beans? (Romans 9:19–21 MSG)

God is not like man, who wants power for selfish reasons or for the luxury that comes with it. He is the power and the luxury already. There is nothing in this world that impresses Him; He created them all. He knows what is best for us because He created us. When you look at nature, there is nothing as wonderful as what He created. Do you realized what a wonderful machine we are? We are able to do so many things consciously and unconsciously. We have a digestive system, a nervous system, an immune system, a hormonal system, a reproductive system, a biological clock and more. All work together so that we can be what we are: human beings.

As we saw in the previous chapter about love, love is the greatest law in our constitution. The history and constitution of our kingdom are written in a book: the Bible. If you are a citizen of a country and don't know your rights, the tendency is that you'll not understand the difference between a refugee, a permanent resident, and you.

A citizen by definition is a member of a state or kingdom, native and naturalized, who owes allegiance to a government and is entitled to protection from it and specified rights and privileges. A refugee is someone who flees or is forced to leave his or her country because of persecution, war, violence, or other reasons. And a permanent resident is someone who has been granted the right to live in a country but has limited rights and privileges. A permanent resident has to be found worthy before being granted citizenship. Ask yourself where you stand. Are you already part of this kingdom? If you are, are you a refugee, a permanent resident, or a citizen? And if you are a citizen, do you know your rights? Your duties? And your privileges?

> But we are citizens of heaven, where the Lord Jesus Christ lives. And we are eagerly waiting for Him to return as our savior. (Philippians 3:20 NLT)

We will not go through every law, rule, or article of our constitution, but I'd just like us to see some key aspects of it.

- Salvation: The way of knowing who you are—a citizen or a queen.

> If you declare with your mouth, "Jesus is Lord," and believe in your heart that God raised him from the dead, you will be saved. For it is with your heart that you believe and are justified, and it is with your mouth that you profess your faith and are saved. (Romans 10:9–10 NIV)

That's it! There is no exam or amount of money required to become a citizen in this kingdom. Salvation is when you decide in your heart to repent and turn away from your sins. You decide to accept Jesus in your heart and accept Him as your Lord and Savior.

> For all have sinned and fall short of the glory of God. (Romans 3:23 NIV)

> Salvation is to be found through him alone; in all the world, there is no one else whom God has given who can save us. (Acts 4:12 NIV)

The Hebrew word translated as salvation in the Old Testament is *yasa*, meaning to save, to deliver, to set free. But in the New Testament, it is the Greek word *sozo*, which means to be made whole, healing, well-being. So when we talk about salvation, Jesus saving us, it means Jesus is forgiving our sins; delivering us from any captivity of the enemy (depression, addiction, homosexuality, rejection, robbery, and so on); saving us from the wickedness of this world; setting us free from any accusations, shame, or chains that had us bound; healing our souls from painful experiences, heartbreaks, bitterness, resentment, anger, wrath, disappointments, and more for our souls are the sieges of our emotions.

> For God saved us and called us to live a holy life. He did this, not because we deserved it, but because that was his plan from before the beginning of time—to show us his grace through Christ Jesus. And now he has made all of this plain to us by the appearing of Christ Jesus, our Savior. He broke the power of death and illuminated the way to life and immortality through the Good News. (2 Timothy 1:9–10 NLT)

In Isaiah 26:1 (NLT), salvation is represented as a wall of protection: "In that day, everyone in the land of Judah will sing this song: Our city is strong! We are surrounded by the walls of God's salvation."

It is true that salvation works as a barrier against the arrows that the enemy shoots at us every single day. Ephesians 6: 17 talks about the helmet of salvation assuredly because the devil is after our minds. The moment he gets our minds, he get our faith, and that's it. For example, he whispers to your mind that you are a good-for-nothing and that God cannot use you because you are full of sin. The moment you believe it, you'll try to run away from your faith. Why are we then still afflicted? Faith.

• Faith

We talked a little bit about faith when we talked about love. Here we will look at faith as the currency of our kingdom.

Currency is the money that a country uses. It is a specific kind of money or something that is used as money. When you need something, like a good or service, you give your money and receive what you asked for.

> Therefore I say unto you, what things soever ye desire, when ye pray, believe (have faith) that ye receive them, and ye shall have them. (Mark 11:24 KJV)

> This Good News tells us how God makes us right in his sight. This is accomplished from start to finish by faith. As the Scriptures say, "It is through faith that a righteous person has life." (Romans 1:17 NLT)

In other words, faith buys righteousness for us, and faith buys us eternal life.

> "You don't have enough faith," Jesus told them. "I tell you the truth, if you had faith even as small as a mustard seed, you could say to this mountain, 'Move from here to there,' and it would move. Nothing would be impossible." (Matthew 17:20 NLT)

So faith buys you power too.

Are you sick? Jesus said to the people He healed, "Go thy faith has healed you."

> Then Jesus said to her, "Woman, you have great faith! Your request is granted." And her daughter was healed at that moment. (Matthew 15:28 NIV)

> Is any sick among you? Let him call for the elders of the church; and let them pray over him, anointing him with oil in the name of the Lord: And the prayer of faith shall save the sick, and the Lord shall raise

him up; and if he has committed sins, they shall be forgiven him. (James 5:14–15 KJV)

It is our faith that makes us to stand and work our salvation with fear and trembling.

So we have been greatly encouraged in the midst of our troubles and suffering, dear brothers and sisters, because you have remained strong in your faith. (1 Thessalonians 3:7 NLT)

Faith gives us victory.

For every child of God defeats this evil world and we achieve this victory through our faith. (1 John 5:4 NLT)

The Bible says without faith we cannot please God. We do not receive because we doubt. We usually say, "If this one doesn't work, then I will use the other one." We work with our understanding and strategies.

But let him ask in faith, nothing wavering. For he that wavereth is like a wave of the sea driven with the wind and tossed. For let not that man think that he shall receive any thing of the Lord. A double minded man is unstable in all his ways. (James 1:6–8 KJV)

• Obedience

This is a word that many of us do not like. I don't know about you, but I remember back in the days when I was a child, my mother would ask me to do something and, she wanted it done by the time she came home. If for any reason I refused to do it, Lord have mercy. I'd be punished— no TV, no games, no nothing. No matter how much I cried she didn't care. But when I did whatever she asked me to do, she gave me almost everything I wanted, according to whether if it was good for me.

Today when I look back, I'm happy that she taught me obedience. The things she was instructing me to do turned out to be for my good. It helped me to stay away from some troubles, and I learned to be independent. Though obviously not independent of God.

That's also how it works in the kingdom of God. He gives us instructions to follow. He expects us to obey them because they are for our own good. It helps us to stay away from trouble. Plus, it is also a sign of love.

> Walk in obedience to all that the Lord has commanded you, so that you may live and prosper and prolong your days in the land that you will possess. (Deuteronomy 5:33 NIV)

And Jesus said, "Anyone who loves me will obey my teaching. My Father will love them and we will come and make our home with them" (John 14:23 NIV).

Obedience is when you yield to explicit instructions or commandments from an authority figure, which in this case is God.

Let's take the example of the police. Whenever we see a police car and we are driving, we double-check to see if we are at the right speed. When we are not, we either try to adjust quickly, or if it is too late, we surrender and stop, waiting for the fine because we know we didn't obey the instructions.

If a police officer, who is made of flesh and blood just like you and me, can have that effect on us, how much more influence does the One who created us and holds our lives in His hands. In just the blink of an eye, He can take it away.

For example, when God tells us not tells us not to have sex before marriage (fornication), it is for our own good. If we all followed that instruction, then we'd not have millions of abortions in the world per day.

King David said, "For you do not desire sacrifice, or else I would give it … the sacrifices of God are a broken spirit, a broken and a contrite heart, these, O God, you will not despise" (Psalm 51:16–17 NKJV).

It is simply because from a broken heart, obedience flows so easily. Obedience is better than sacrifice.

Even Jesus had to be obedient. He purposely came in the flesh to show us that it is possible.

> Though he was God, he did not think of equality with God as something to cling to. Instead, he gave up his divine privileges; he took the humble position of a slave and was born as a human being. When he appeared in human form, he humbled himself in obedience to God and died a criminal's death on a cross. (Philippians 2:6–8 NLT)

Obedience is one of the key elements in our constitution. Obedience is to submit to God and believe that He knows what is best, even when we don't understand why.

• Authority

It is very important to understand the authority that has been given to us through Christ Jesus. As children of God, being queens in the kingdom comes with authority (Colossians 1:12–13 NLT; 1 Peter 2:9 NLT).

> Little children (believers, dear ones), you are of God and you belong to Him and have [already] overcome

them [the agents of the antichrist]; because He who
is in you is greater than he (Satan) who is in the world
[of sinful mankind]. (1 John 4:4 AMP)

Authority is the power or right to give orders, make decisions, and
enforce obedience.

One of the reasons many of us who already believe in Christ live a
defeated life in depression, poverty, sickness, are bound, or can't get
rid of an addiction is because we have no idea of the authority we have.

And hast made us unto our God kings and priests:
and we shall reign on the earth. (Revelation 5:10 KJV)

Do you see that? We shall reign on the earth, not in heaven. How
many of us can boldly testify that we are reigning on this earth?

When you go to verse 12 of that same chapter, it says, "Worthy is
the Lamb that was slain to receive power (authority), and riches,
and wisdom, and strength, and honor, and glory and blessing." As
my spiritual Father explains it so well, He didn't receive these things
for Himself. He already had them even before the foundation of
the world. No, He received it for us. He gave us power, authority
to overcome, to bind and loose, to cast out, to decree a thing and it
comes to pass.

We have authority

    a.   To overcome

        Little children (believers, dear ones), you are of God
        and you belong to Him and have [already] overcome
        them [the agents of the Antichrist]; because He who
        is in you is greater than he (Satan) who is in the world
        [of sinful humankind]. (1 John 4:4 AMP)

Jesus lives in us, and the one who is in this world is the devil and all his agents. They represent sickness, poverty, affliction, depression, and so on.

> And Christ lives within you, so even though your body will die because of sin, the Spirit gives you life because you have been made right with God. The Spirit of God, who raised Jesus from the dead, lives in you. And just as God raised Christ Jesus from the dead, he will give life to your mortal bodies by this same Spirit living within you. (Romans 8:10–11 NLT)

The same power that resurrected Christ from death lives inside us. You still doubt? I'm not the one saying it; it's in the Word. So why don't we see that power manifesting?

b. To decree a thing, and it comes to pass.

> But Peter said, "I don't have any silver or gold for you. But I'll give you what I have. In the name of Jesus Christ the Nazarene, get up and walk!" Then Peter took the lame man by the right hand and helped him up. And as he did, the man's feet and ankles were instantly healed and strengthened. (Acts 3:6 NLT)

c. To bind and to loose

Verily I say unto you, whatsoever ye shall bind on earth shall be bound in heaven, and whatsoever ye shall loose on earth shall be loosed in heaven. Again I say unto you, that if two of you shall agree on earth as touching anything that they shall ask, it shall be done for them of my Father which is in heaven. (Matthew 18:18–19 NLT)

d. To cast out demons

Giving them authority to cast out demons. (Mark 3:15 NLT)

These miraculous signs will accompany those who believe: They will cast out demons in my name. (Mark 16:17–18 NLT)

   e. To tread upon serpents

Behold, I give unto you power to tread on serpents and scorpions, and over all the power of the enemy: and nothing shall by any means hurt you. (Luke 10:19 KJV)

Prayer:

I would like to share with you a story that has always encouraged me, especially in times of discouragements.

This is the story of a woman of God who gave her life to Christ many years ago and was ordained pastor at a certain point in her Christian life, got married and had children. A moment came when her first daughter decided to convert to a Muslim. You can imagine people talking about it: *she is a pastor and her daughter is a Muslim? What kind of God does she serve? She failed as a Christian mother or she must have sin and God is now punishing her.*

She got to a point where she had to ask herself: *where do I go from here? I do not have any strength of my own. The only thing I have left is to call on the One who gave her to me; I will pray.*

I can still remember the look on her face when she was telling us her story. You could feel in between her words that she went through tears and pain. But she said: *it is then, that I realized that I should pray like I have never done before. I cried to God day and night for my daughter to get back to Jesus. But the more I was praying, the more she* will get committed in her Muslim faith. I could not abandon. I had to believe God that no matter what reality could show me, He was able to save. Though I was in tears, I kept on praying. After all, I had been the one preaching about the power of prayer and faith. It was my time to put that word in practice. Then, on that faithful day, when I was least expecting it, she asked me if she could come with me for a Christian program we had. After that, she kept on making baby steps to get back to her Christian faith.

And that is how her prayer got answered after many years.

Praying is having a conversation with God; to tell him about our gratitude, our worries, our emotions, our weaknesses, our temptations and everything that we can think of. It is through prayer that the impossible becomes possible; it is through prayer that we get closer to God to hear his mind and plans for us, just as Jesus, the bible says, was constantly withdrawing himself to pray.

Matthew 26:41 tells us that it is through prayer that we shall resist temptations.

Matthew 21:22 and Philippians 4:6 talk about the prayer of faith to receive from God what we have been requesting.

1 Timothy 2: 1 talks about prayer of intercession for others.

James 5: 17 one my favorites, says:

> Elias was a man subject to like passions as we are, and he prayed earnestly that it might not rain: and it rained not on the earth by the space of three years and six months. (KJV)

> 1 Thessalonians 1: 17 always exhorts us to persevere in prayer. Just as in the story of the woman of God, it is by perseverance that we will breakthrough in

this world. This brings me to two specifics points in prayer:

• Spiritual warfare

> For the weapons of our warfare are not carnal, but mighty through God to the pulling down of strong holds;) Casting down imaginations, and every high thing that exalteth itself against the knowledge of God, and bringing into captivity every thought to the obedience of Christ. (2 Corinthians 10:4–5 KJV)

In these verses, it is not written as if warfare were optional. It doesn't say, "If you are in warfare, then use the weapons." Whether we like it or not, we are in warfare. There is a battle and a battlefield.

> For we[d] are not fighting against flesh-and-blood enemies, but against evil rulers and authorities of the unseen world, against mighty powers in this dark world, and against evil spirits in the heavenly places. (Ephesians 6:10–12 NLT)

Those evil rulers and evil spirits are the ones fighting our destinies and purposes for God. They attack our minds, our finances, our families, our jobs, our relationships, and every other thing they can use to bring us down.

> The thief comes only in order to steal and kill and destroy. I came that they may have and enjoy life, and have it in abundance [to the full, till it overflows]. (John 10:10 AMP)

He wants to destroy without mercy, to divide families, to cause war among nations, to afflict us with every kind of disease, to promote sexual immorality, and to cause death, famine, and more.

First Peter 5:8–9 (AMP) says,

> Be sober [well balanced and self-disciplined], be alert and cautious at all times. That enemy of yours, the devil, prowls around like a roaring lion [fiercely hungry], seeking someone to devour. But resist him, be firm in your faith [against his attack—rooted, established, immovable], knowing that the same experiences of suffering are being experienced by your brothers and sisters throughout the world. [You do not suffer alone.]

- Intercession

Intercession is the pleading or intervening on behalf of somebody else. It can also be seen as mediation, arbitration, conciliation, or negotiation. In fact, when you intercede, you petition on behalf of someone else's case. This English word is derived from the Latin *intercede*, which means "to come between."

Along the same line, to advocate is defined as to speak in favor of, to support by argument, to act as an advocate, and to plead for or on behalf of another.

In other words to intercede is just like to advocate. An intercessor can be described as an advocate. It's like playing the peacemaker between two or more parties.

Remember the story of Queen Esther? A decree was passed against the Jews, and they were to be killed. She first took the case to the greatest judge, who is the King of kings, and then to King Xerxès (Esther 5:2, 6–8 KJV).

Queen Esther carried the burdens of the Jews upon her. Her intercession could cost her life, but she went ahead.

> And I sought for a man among them, that should
> make up the hedge, and stand in the gap before me
> for the land, that I should not destroy it: but I found
> none. (Ezekiel 22:30 KJV)

In our kingdom, intercession is a necessity. We are each other's keepers. Nobody is strong enough to stand by himself or herself. We intercede not only for ourselves as believers but especially for those who are still in ignorance and in captivity. If you remember, we said in the first chapter that one of the characteristics of a queen is the "desire to reunite." A queen should be a peacemaker, a reconciliatory, an ambassador representing our kingdom on this earth.

> and gave us the ministry of reconciliation: that God
> was reconciling the world to himself in Christ, not
> counting people's sins against them. And he has
> committed to us the message of reconciliation. (2
> Corinthians 5:17–21 NIV)

Jesus is our greatest intercessor; He reconciled us back to God. For though we were sinners and condemned to death, He became a mediator, an intercessor, pleading for us right to the point of dying on the cross so that the great King, the Lord of Hosts, would not destroy us in His anger. Like in Ezekiel 22, which we just read, Jesus made up the hedge and stood in the gap for us. And because we are of the same kingdom, it is a duty for us reconciled people—drug addicts, adulterers, robbers, murderers, homosexuals, drunkards, rapists, and all those called wicked or evil, basically all the lost souls—to God. We intercede so none should perish but should be saved. We plead for them before God, so that He will do a new thing in their lives.

> My dear children, I write this to you so that you will
> not sin. But if anybody does sin, we have an advocate
> with the Father—Jesus Christ, the Righteous One.
> He is the atoning sacrifice for our sins, and not only

for ours but also for the sins of the whole world. (1 John 2:1–2 NIV)

One of my favorite scriptures about intercession is Jeremiah 9:17–22 (MSG). When we see the natural disasters occurring all around, we can only see the wrath of God in it. Is God wicked? Of course not! But the people have turned their backs on Him and departed far from Him. People do evil things, ready to kill their neighbors for the sake of money. Some of them rape little children. Some kill their own families. So many evil and abominable things. But we, as queens and daughters of the King of kings, can come in and play peacemakers. We come between God and the people of this world, and we plead on their behalf. We ask Him to forgive their sins as well as ours.

> Look over the trouble we're in and call for help. Send for some singers who can help us mourn our loss. Tell them to hurry—to help us express our loss and lament, help us get our tears flowing, make tearful music of our crying. Listen to it! Listen to that torrent of tears out of Zion … Death has climbed in through the window, broken into our bedrooms. Children on the playgrounds drop dead and young men and women collapse at their games. Speak up! (Jeremiah 9:17–21 MSG)

The desire of the Father is that people shall turn from their wicked ways. You and I were not born perfect and without sin; we do our own evil things, our own sins. Yet He saved us, not because we worked for it, lest we should boast that we were saved by our own abilities. "For by grace are ye saved through faith; and that not of yourselves: it is the gift of God: Not of works, lest any man should boast (Ephesians 2:8–9 KJV). Somebody somewhere prayed for us.

A queen seeks to reunite, reconcile, and see people saved. She carries the burden of the kingdom at heart. That is why intercession is important. For the day of the Lord is at hand, Nations are going against nations, people are so selfish that they do not care about their neighbors, and people are ready to kill for money and power. But all those things were written about and will come to pass.

> You should know this, Timothy that in the last days there will be very difficult times. For people will love only themselves and their money. They will be boastful and proud, scoffing at God, disobedient to their parents, and ungrateful. They will consider nothing sacred. They will be unloving and unforgiving; they will slander others and have no self-control. They will be cruel and hate what is good. They will betray their friends, be reckless, be puffed up with pride, and love pleasure rather than God. They will act religious, but they will reject the power that could make them godly. (2 Timothy 3:1–9 NLT)

Watch the news, and tell me if you don't see these things happening. But we should keep this in mind:

> But you must not forget this one thing, dear friends: A day is like a thousand years to the Lord, and a thousand years is like a day. The Lord isn't really being slow about his promise, as some people think. No, he is being patient for your sake. He does not want anyone to be destroyed, but wants everyone to repent. But the day of the Lord will come as unexpectedly as a thief. Then the heavens will pass away with a terrible noise, and the very elements themselves will disappear in fire, and the earth and everything on it will be found to deserve judgment. (2 Peter 3:8–10 NLT)

To sit and think about our own problems, meditate on how people betrayed and hurt us, is selfish. I remember when I just came to the

Lord and was so afraid of my destiny, afraid of all the prophesies that I was receiving about my calling. I said, "I can't do this. It is too much for me. I already have my own trouble I need to deal with." And the Holy Spirit said to me, "It is selfishness that makes you speak this way. For your eyes are only on yourself, and you don't see the lost souls who are patiently waiting that you should, by answering to your calling, help them to come out of the darkness." And since that day, I stopped complaining and just decided to patiently endure the process.

Second Chronicles 7:14 (KJV) says, "If my people, which are called by my name, shall humble themselves, and pray, and seek my face, and turn from their wicked ways; then will I hear from heaven, and will forgive their sin, and will heal their land."

Remember Isaiah 43, which we read earlier in the book. It said, "I have called you by your name, Thou are mine." We are His; we are His people. So this verse is talking about us. If we can humble ourselves and pray and seek His face; intercede on behalf of nations; reconcile man to God, telling them to repent and turn back to God because He is the way out of our mess; the truth in our ignorance and the life when we are dead; then God will surely answer.

Going through the Process

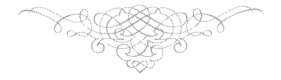

Dear friends, don't be surprised at the fiery trials you are going through, as if something strange were happening to you …

If you suffer, however, it must not be for murder, stealing, making trouble, or prying into other people's affair.

1 Peter 4:12, 15 NLT

In this life we live, it is impossible to avoid struggles. There are financial, emotional, mental, physical, familial struggles, and more. We all go through at least one of them if not all.

Going through the process of becoming who the Almighty wants you to be—a queen—is not without trials or persecutions and storms. Some people believe that once you give your life to Christ, as He makes you a queen, you will not have any struggles, everything will be all rosy, you will eat on a platter of gold, or even just wish for something and have it given to you. Sounds good. Once in heaven, maybe, but not on this earth. Forget it. As we saw in the scriptures above, it is not strange that we go through trials.

But there are sufferings that we bring upon ourselves that have nothing to do with the process. Like apostle Paul wrote, putting your nose into someone else business, for example.

We all have a purpose in this life. Nobody was born to come to this world to study and struggle to have a job, pay bills, build a family (which might even be unstable), and die.

Going through this journey is necessary regardless of your past or what the reality of this world shows us.

As we said in the introduction, the making of a queen is a process, and it takes time.

- Time to acknowledge that you are on the wrong way. Turn away and do not go back.

A $50 bill that is kept in one of the most expensive wallets is not more valuable than one lost in a bush or in the forest. What makes the difference is the fact that the one in the expensive wallet knows its value, while the one in the forest doesn't know because nobody is using it.

Or better still, an eagle that was raised among chickens is the same in identity as one that is soaring high in the air. The difference is that the one raised among chickens will see itself as a chick and not have any idea that it has an ability to soar very high and has better qualities than chickens—until it realizes that it is in the wrong place, leaves that place, learns to soar high and never go back to the chicken yard. Not that the eagle will hate the chicken, but it will then understand that it was not created to be there. An eagle will never be a chicken.

It is the same for us. We were born as princesses, but many of us do not know our identities because we happen to be in the wrong yard and do not realize it. It's when you realize that you are living in sin, are tired of that life, and come to Christ that you discover that, in fact, you were like the eagle among chickens. At that moment, you will need to leave that chicken yard and decide to be trained as the eagle you are. It is when you get to know the King that you discover the princess in you.

- Time to be healed and to be restored.

The Woman at the Well

> To get there, he had to pass through Samaria. He came into Sychar, a Samaritan village that bordered the field Jacob had given his son Joseph. Jacob's well was still there. Jesus, worn out by the trip, sat down at the well. It was noon. A woman, a Samaritan, came to draw water. Jesus said, "Would you give me a drink of water?" (His disciples had gone to the village to buy food for lunch.) … Jesus said, "Everyone who drinks this water will get thirsty again and again. Anyone who drinks the water I give will never thirst—not ever. "It's who you are and the way you live that count before God. Your worship must engage your spirit in the pursuit of truth." (John 4:4–10, 13, 23, 28–30 MSG)

We all have a past, bad experiences, heartbreaks, trauma, and shameful experiences. We all come from somewhere, and the pains and wounds of our past experiences, along with the shame, stay in our memories and as scars in our souls.

There is a healing of the body that's for sicknesses or diseases. And there is the healing of the soul that has to do with restoration from the inside, taking away the sorrows, pains, shame, and tears that came with the past.

In this story, we see a woman who carried her own baggage. She had five husbands; she went through the pain of separation and divorce four times. She was surely judged, rejected, and condemned by others because of her story. When she met Jesus at the well, He said, "I would give you fresh, living water." He knew her past, her story, and what she was going through. He said, "everyone who drinks this water will get thirsty again and again. Anyone who drinks the water I give will never thirst, not ever" (John 4:13-14).

The water of the well is good for body cleansing, but that "fresh, living water" cleanses and heals your soul. It washes away depression and the pain of rejection, trauma, shame, guilt, emotional wounds, and scars. There is a need of restoration when we are going through this process. Drink of this living water, and be healed and restored.

What is this living water? The Word of God.

The Woman with the Alabaster Box

> And, behold, a woman in the city, which was a sinner, when she knew that Jesus sat at meat in the Pharisee's house, brought an alabaster box of ointment, and stood at his feet behind him weeping, and began to wash his feet with tears, and did wipe them with the hairs of her head, and kissed his feet, and anointed them with the ointment. Now when the Pharisee which had bidden him saw it, he spake within himself, saying, This man, if he were a prophet, would have known who and what manner of woman this is that toucheth him: for she is a sinner … And he said to the woman, Thy faith hath saved thee; go in peace. (Luke 7:37–39, 44–50 KJV)

They found a name for her: a sinner. That's how she was identified because of her past, because of the wrong choices she made, the bad experiences she had. They titled her a sinner.

Many of us have kept bitterness in our hearts and souls because of our pasts. Because people keep identifying us with our pasts, it keeps us in that place of bondage. But I declare that as you are reading this book, the Lord is restoring you and healing your soul.

Because her pains were too much, instead of thinking of committing suicide or waste her time justifying herself, she went to the Master's feet. She understood that He was the One to take that pain away, the One to restore her and free her from the bondage she was in. She fell at his feet. She washed His feet with her tears, the tears she used to shed for people who didn't recognized or couldn't see the queen in her. She wiped them with her hair, which the Bible describes as a woman's glory according to 1 Corinthians 11:15, and she anointed his feet.

"And he said to the woman, Thy faith hath saved thee; go in peace." The Greek word for "saved" in this passage is "sozo," which means healed, restored, and made whole. In other words, Jesus was telling the woman, "Your faith has healed you, restored you, and made you whole."

At the feet of Jesus, she humbled herself, surrendered to Him, believed that He could heal her from emotional pain, and was restored.

The Woman with the Issue of Blood

> And a certain woman, which had an issue of blood twelve years, and had suffered many things of many physicians, and had spent all that she had, and was nothing bettered, but rather grew worse, when she had heard of Jesus, came in the press behind, and touched

his garment ... "And he said unto her, Daughter, thy
faith hath made thee whole; go in peace, and be whole
of thy plague." (Mark 5:25–34 KJV)

For twelve years this woman struggled with an issue of blood, for
twelve good years. She went from physician to physician and could
not be healed. She spent all her money, and it went from bad to worst.
For twelve years. Maybe she was discouraged at a point; maybe she
had nobody to assist her. But when she heard that Jesus was around,
she thought, *If I could only touch His clothes I shall be whole.* She
understood that Jesus was the solution, the One who could heal her.

So she humbled herself before the Master, and He said to her,
"Daughter, thy faith hath made thee whole; go in peace, and be whole
of thy plague."

And she was healed.

Queen Esther

As we saw when we were talking about Queen Esther, twelve months
of treatment were required before any young woman could meet the
king. We saw how that process was for restoration, wholeness, and
beautification.

> Before each young woman was taken to the king's
> bed, she was given the prescribed twelve months of
> beauty treatments—six months with oil of myrrh,
> followed by six months with special perfumes and
> ointment. (Esther 2:12 NLT)

This process ensured a wholeness that started from the inside and
went to the outside.

What the society is doing today is to cover up. It makes us focus on
what is external and superficial, our outward appearance. But the

truth is, it starts from the inside to radiate on the outside. There is a need of healing of the soul and the body, a need of being made whole so that you can stand confident in who the Lord says that you are. Your self-esteem increases, and you are freed from every pain, bitterness, unforgiveness, resentment, malice, and more. A queen is first beautiful from the inside and then on the outside.

Take time to be healed at Jesus's feet. Ask the Lord to heal you from every pain of the past so that you can be 100 percent when He calls you to be a queen.

- Time to cherish and nurture a relationship.

When you discover your identity, building a solid relationship is necessary. Consider that you are an adopted child who, after many years, finally finds out that you have been adopted. The first reflex is to want to know who your biological parents are. You will go around looking for them, and once you find them (assuming they are still alive), you'll try to understand why you ended up in another family. You'll likely try to keep that relationship with your biological parents even though sometimes it is painful.

Now let's say you find out that this happened because at your birth, there was a switch, or somebody stole you to give you to another family in exchange of a great amount of money. One thing that will happen is that you will do your best to get even closer to your biological parents because you realize that they are your flesh and blood. They brought you into this world. You have things in common, things that you never understood where they came from. And you will want to know more about your family, especially your parents.

When you discover and understand that your Father is the King of kings, one thing you'll need is to get closer to Him. He has the answers to every question you have. How far you will go or how

The Making of a Queen

successful you will be in this kingdom depends on how well you cherish and nurture your relationship with the Father.

King David said, "One thing have I desired of the Lord, that will I seek after; that I may dwell in the house of the Lord all the days of my life, to behold the beauty of the Lord, and to enquire in his temple" (Psalm 27:4 KJV).

David was already a king. He had every material riches that could be. But he understood that the One who was holding his kingship and making him to reign and rule was far more important than all that he had. He was after a relationship. David was called a man after God's heart.

> And when he had removed him, he raised up unto them David to be their king; to whom also he gave their testimony, and said, I have found David the son of Jesse, a man after mine own heart, which shall fulfil all my will. (Acts 13:22 KJV)

David is an example of someone who cherished and nurtured that relationship with the Father.

Take note of these verses and meditate on it as you read them.

> I will love thee, O Lord, my strength. The Lord is my rock, and my fortress, and my deliverer; my God, my strength, in whom I will trust; my buckler, and the horn of my salvation, and my high tower. I will call upon the Lord, who is worthy to be praised: so shall I be saved from mine enemies. (Psalm 18:1–3 KJV)

> I will praise you, Lord, with all my heart; I will tell of all the marvelous things you have done. I will be filled

with joy because of you. I will sing praises to your name, O Most High. (Psalm 9:1–2 NLT)

I have seen you in your sanctuary and gazed upon your power and glory. Your unfailing love is better than life itself; how I praise you! I will praise you as long as I live, lifting up my hands to you in prayer. You satisfy me more than the richest feast. I will praise you with songs of joy. I lie awake thinking of you, meditating on you through the night. Because you are my helper, I sing for joy in the shadow of your wings. I cling to you; your strong right hand holds me securely. (Psalm 63:2–8 NLT)

Lead me to the towering rock of safety, for you are my safe refuge, a fortress where my enemies cannot reach me. Let me live forever in your sanctuary, safe beneath the shelter of your wings! (Psalm 61:2–4 NLT)

But as for me, I will sing about your power. Each morning I will sing with joy about your unfailing love. For you have been my refuge, a place of safety when I am in distress. (Psalm 59:16 NLT)

O Lord, you have examined my heart and know everything about me. You know when I sit down or stand up. You know my thoughts even when I'm far away. You see me when I travel and when I rest at home. You know everything I do. You know what I am going to say even before I say it, Lord. You go before me and follow me. You place your hand of blessing on my head. Such knowledge is too wonderful for me, too great for me to understand! (Psalm 139:1–6 NLT)

Those kinds of words can only come from a heart of somebody who loves and cherishes the relationship with the Father. Let's learn to build a relationship with the almighty King, and He will strengthen us in time of need.

The Lord said in the book of Jeremiah, "If you look for me wholeheartedly, you will find me. I will be found by you" (Jeremiah 29:13–14 NLT).

The Father is open to have a relationship with us. He is not a wicked Father. "Look! I stand at the door and knock. If you hear my voice and open the door, I will come in, and we will share a meal together as friends" (Revelation 3:20 NLT).

- Time to fall and to stand up.

Nobody knows. Sometimes you can be so sure of something until you are proved wrong. Apostle Paul said, "Wherefore let him that thinketh he standeth take heed lest he fall" (1 Corinthians 10:12 KJV).

You will never understand this until you fall so low that you ask yourself, "What have I done? Will I be able to stand up again?"

You fall so low that you cry; you shed tears of guilt, shame, and fear, but most important, tears of repentance.

You fall so low that the people around you can't really help. You are hurt by hurting Him. You fall so low and so bad, you look around and wonder, *What can I do?* So you just cry.

And suddenly, you hear that still small voice whispering to you and telling you, "I'll never forsake you nor abandon you. So come, come boldly; come to my throne of grace to obtain mercy and find help in time of need. Come as the prodigal son."

Apostle Paul said,

Sin is no longer your master, for you no longer live under the requirements of the law. Instead, you live under the freedom of God's grace. Well then, since God's grace has set us free from the law, does that mean we can go on sinning? Of course not! Don't you realize that you become the slave of whatever you choose to obey? You can be a slave to sin, which leads to death, or you can choose to obey God, which leads to righteous living. (Romans 6:14–16 NLT)

I have discovered this principle of life—that when I want to do what is right, I inevitably do what is wrong. I love God's law with all my heart. But there is another power within me that is at war with my mind. This power makes me a slave to the sin that is still within me. Oh, what a miserable person I am! Who will free me from this life that is dominated by sin and death? Thank God! The answer is in Jesus Christ our Lord. So you see how it is: In my mind I really want to obey God's law, but because of my sinful nature I am a slave to sin. (Romans 7:21–25 NLT)

So what are we saying? Is it okay to keep on falling or sinning? No. Can you or will you make mistakes? Yes. Do you have to live in guilt and shame because of that? No. But it comes back to what we were saying in the previous point. When you have a close relationship with Him, you will hate and despise what is not like Him: "This I say then, Walk in the Spirit, and ye shall not fulfil the lust of the flesh" (Galatians 5:16 KJV).

King David, like we saw before, had a repentant heart though he sinned against God. He understood it was wrong, repented, moved ahead, and never went back to it. He said, "Thy word have I hid in mine heart, that I might not sin against thee" (Psalm 119:11 KJV). It was because of his love for God that he had the fear of God.

So when we fall, we should learn how to stand up and move on. It is written in 2 Corinthians 12:9 (KJV), "My grace is sufficient for thee: for my strength is made perfect in weakness."

Take time to read and study the parable of the prodigal son (Luke 15:11–32). Let the Lord reveal to you the depth of His love that provides us grace to run back to Him even when we have done foolishly. Rather, He wants to hold our hands to take us out of any mess we find ourselves in. His love never fails.

- Time to hear and obey.

    As Jesus was saying these things, a woman in the crowd called out, "Blessed is the mother who gave you birth and nursed you." He replied, "Blessed rather are those who hear the word of God and obey it." (Luke 11:28 NIV)

When we were looking at the biblical examples of queens, we talked about how Ruth was obedient to her mother-in-law as well as Esther was with her cousin Mordecai. It's important to listen to what the Father is saying and obey it.

    But don't just listen to God's word. You must do what it says. Otherwise, you are only fooling yourselves. (James 1:22 NLT)

Somebody might ask, "How can I hear the voice of God?" Well, God speaks in many different ways to different people. But the fundamental way is through the Word, the Bible. You don't only read it, you practice what you read. And we also have shepherds and spiritual leaders like Naomi or Mordecai whom God puts in our way so that they can lead us; they will be as His mouthpiece. Then when we get deeper into the spiritual things, you will learn to hear Him by yourself.

My sheep listen to my voice; I know them, and they follow me. I give them eternal life, and they will never perish. No one can snatch them away from me. (John 10:27–28 NLT)

If you fully obey the Lord your God and carefully keep all his commands that I am giving you today, the Lord your God will set you high above all the nations of the world. (Deuteronomy 28:1 NLT)

- Time to sacrifice.

There is something that is inevitable in this process: sacrifice.

In the story of Ruth, she sacrificed all that she had in the land of Moab. The journey cost her the loss of her husband. She followed Naomi to a land where strangers were not very welcome. She sacrificed her time by going to a glen in Boaz' farm, and that's how she got her breakthrough.

In this process, you will have to sacrifice something, either time or money or energy or relationships. Perhaps even your life. "For whoever wants to save their life will lose it, but whoever loses their life for me will save it" (Luke 9:24 NIV).

Let's look at the story of Joseph, Jacob's son.

> This is the account of Jacob and his family. When Joseph was seventeen years old, he often tended his father's flocks. He worked for his half-brothers, the sons of his father's wives Bilhah and Zilpah. But Joseph reported to his father some of the bad things his brothers were doing. Jacob loved Joseph more than any of his other children because Joseph had been born to him in his old age. So one day Jacob had a

special gift made for Joseph—a beautiful robe. But his brothers hated Joseph because their father loved him more than the rest of them. They couldn't say a kind word to him. One night Joseph had a dream, and when he told his brothers about it, they hated him more than ever. "Listen to this dream," he said. "We were out in the field, tying up bundles of grain. Suddenly my bundle stood up, and your bundles all gathered around and bowed low before mine!" His brothers responded, "So you think you will be our king, do you? Do you actually think you will reign over us?" And they hated him all the more because of his dreams and the way he talked about them. (Genesis 37:2–8 NLT)

When Joseph had his dreams, he didn't know that this was the beginning of his journey to become who God wanted him to be.

When Joseph's brothers saw him coming, they recognized him in the distance. As he approached, they made plans to kill him. "Here comes the dreamer!" they said. "Come on, let's kill him and throw him into one of these cisterns. We can tell our father, 'A wild animal has eaten him.' Then we'll see what becomes of his dreams!" (Genesis 37:18–20 NLT)

His making cost him the hatred of his brothers, who sold him into slavery.

In Genesis 39 we find,

When Joseph was taken to Egypt by the Ishmaelite traders, he was purchased by Potiphar, an Egyptian officer. Potiphar was captain of the guard for Pharaoh, the king of Egypt. The Lord was with Joseph, so he succeeded in everything he did as he served in the home of his Egyptian master. Potiphar noticed this and realized that the Lord was with Joseph; giving him success in everything he did ... So Potiphar gave Joseph complete administrative responsibility over everything he owned. With Joseph there, he didn't worry about a thing—except what kind of food to eat! Joseph was a very handsome and well-built young man, and Potiphar's wife soon began to look at him lustfully. "Come and sleep with me," she demanded. But Joseph refused. "Look," he told her, "my master trusts me with everything in his entire household." (Genesis 39:1–3, 6–8 NLT)

Do you think that Joseph was not man enough to have sexual needs and temptations? Of course not. But he understood what loyalty and royalty were all about. Loyalty toward his master because he knew his master trusted him, and he was there to serve. Royalty because he knew it would be evil before the almighty King. And even at that, he was put in prison because Potiphar's wife lied against him.

But the Lord was with Joseph in the prison and showed him his faithful love. And the Lord made Joseph a favorite with the prison warden. (Genesis 39:16–21 NLT)

The Lord was with Joseph, yet he was in prison. Am I dreaming? Just imagine for a moment that you have just done something so good that you are proud of and you tell yourself: *I didn't fall, I stood my ground. it is the Lord that will bless me for that.* But rather, you are put in jail and the Lord tells you he will give you favor in jail. Honestly speaking, the first words that are going to proceed out of a mouth are: It Is Not Fair. How can God allow it to happen to me? I am such a good person. Well, it is good to understand that because you are facing difficulties, it doesn't mean God is not with you, especially if it is for His sake. There is no way you are going to stand for royal/ kingdom principles according to our constitution and the Lord not back you up. When you sacrifice your life, your time, and whatever for Him, He surely sees and will show you His faithful love. Joseph became the second most powerful person in Egypt after Pharaoh. From slave to governor.

- Time to get hurt and forgive.

  So Joseph's ten older brothers went down to Egypt to buy grain. But Jacob wouldn't let Joseph's younger brother, Benjamin, go with them, for fear some harm might come to him. So Jacob's sons arrived in Egypt along with others to buy food, for the famine was in Canaan as well. Since Joseph was governor of all Egypt and in charge of selling grain to all the people, it was to him that his brothers came. When they arrived, they bowed before him with their faces to the ground. Joseph recognized his brothers instantly, but he pretended to be a stranger and spoke harshly to them. "Where are you from?" he demanded. "From the land of Canaan," they replied. "We have come to buy food." Although Joseph recognized his brothers, they didn't recognize him. And he remembered the dreams he'd had about them many years before. He said to them, "You are spies! You have come to see how vulnerable our land has become." So Joseph put them all in prison for three days. On the third day Joseph said to them, "I am a God-fearing man. If you do as I say, you will live. If you really are honest men, choose one of your brothers to remain in prison. The rest of you may go home with grain for your starving families. But you must bring your youngest brother back to me. This will prove that you are telling the truth, and you will not die." To this they agreed. Speaking among themselves, they said, "Clearly we are being punished because of what we did to Joseph long ago. We saw his anguish when he pleaded for his life, but we wouldn't listen. That's why we're in this trouble." "Didn't I tell you not to sin against the boy?" Reuben asked. "But you wouldn't listen. And now we have to answer for his blood!" Of course, they didn't know that Joseph understood them, for he had been speaking to them through an interpreter. Now he turned away from them and began to weep. When he regained his composure, he spoke to them again. Then he chose Simeon from among them and had him tied up right before their eyes ... When the brothers came to their father, Jacob, in the land of Canaan, they told him everything that had happened to them. "The man who is governor of the land spoke very harshly to us," they told him. "He accused us of being spies scouting the land. But we said, 'We are honest men, not spies. We are twelve brothers, sons of one father. One brother is no longer with us, and the youngest is at home with our father in the land of Canaan.' "Then the man who is governor of the land told us, 'This is how I will find out if you are honest men. Leave one of your brothers here with me, and take grain for your starving families and go on home.'" (Genesis 42:3–9, 17–23, 29–33 NLT)

Joseph could stand it no longer. There were many people in the room, and he said to his attendants, "Out, all of you!" So he was alone with his brothers when he told them who he was. Then he broke down and wept. He wept so loudly the Egyptians could hear him, and word of it quickly carried to Pharaoh's palace. "I am Joseph!" he said to his brothers. "Is my father still alive?" But his brothers were speechless! They were stunned to realize that Joseph was standing there in front of them. "Please, come closer," he said to them. So they came closer. And he said again, "I am Joseph, your brother, whom you sold into slavery in Egypt. But don't be upset, and don't be angry with yourselves for selling me to this place. It was God who sent me here ahead of you to preserve your lives. This famine that has ravaged the land for two years will last five more years and there will be neither plowing nor harvesting. God has sent me ahead of you to keep you and your families alive and to preserve many survivors. So it was God who sent me here, not you! And he is the one who made me an adviser to Pharaoh—the manager of his entire palace and the governor of all Egypt ... Then Joseph added, "Look! You can see for yourselves, and so can my brother Benjamin, that I really am Joseph! Go tell my father of my honored position here in Egypt. Describe for him everything you have seen, and then bring my father here quickly." Weeping with joy, he embraced Benjamin, and Benjamin did the same. Then Joseph kissed each of his brothers and wept over them, and after that they began talking freely with him. (Genesis 45:1–8, 12–15 NLT)

Joseph was sold in slavery by his brothers, and he went to prison for something he had not done. At this point, some of us would already start complaining, "Lord, why? Do You really exist? An injustice is done to me, and You are watching?" Some of us will just start binding that demon: "You evil spirits against my success catch fire in Jesus's name." Some will start accusing the people around them of being witches and wizards.

Joseph experienced great pain. It hurts to know that the people you love and trust are the very ones who want to see you dead. But it is that pain and betrayal that led him to his destiny. (To fully understand the story, read Genesis 37 to Genesis 45). When confronted with a situation that he could use to take his revenge, he chose to forgive. Not only that, he asked them to forgive themselves as well and invited them to share his riches. Some of us would have said, "Well, I forgave them, but I don't want to have anything to do with them. Let them stay where they are, and I will stay in my own corner."

Remember we talked about how love doesn't keep records but forgives. That is exactly what Joseph did.

> "Please, come closer," he said to them. So they came closer. And he said again, "I am Joseph, your brother, whom you sold into slavery in Egypt. But don't be upset, and don't be angry with yourselves for selling me to this place. It was God who sent me here ahead of you to preserve your lives … Then Joseph kissed each of his brothers and wept over them, and after that they began talking freely with him. (Genesis 45:4–5, 15 NLT)

Joseph understood that the pain of betrayal was for divine purpose. In this life, we will all get hurt. But as we do, we should forgive and understand as it is written in Romans 8:28 (KJV): "And we know that all things work together for good to them that love God, to them who are the called according to his purpose."

Don't let the pain that comes with the purpose of your life cause you to live in darkness with unforgiveness, bitterness, and more, and then stop you from receiving your promise.

- Time to trust and to be betrayed.

In the same line with time to be hurt and forgive, there is also a time to trust and be betrayed. We saw how Joseph was betrayed by his brothers, who he trusted and loved. I want us to look at another example of betrayal.

> Some time later Samson fell in love with a woman named Delilah, who lived in the valley of Sorek. The rulers of the Philistines went to her and said, "Entice Samson to tell you what makes him so strong and how he can be overpowered and tied up securely. Then each of us will give you 1,100 pieces of silver." (…) Finally, Samson shared his secret with her. "My hair has never been cut," he confessed, "for I was dedicated to God as a Nazirite from birth. If my head were shaved, my strength would leave me, and I would become as weak as anyone else." Delilah realized he had finally told her the truth, so she sent for the Philistine rulers. "Come back one more time," she said, "for he has finally told me his secret." So the Philistine rulers returned with the money in their hands. Delilah lulled Samson to sleep with his head in her lap, and then she called in a man to shave off the seven locks of his hair. In this way she began to bring him down, and his strength left him. Then she cried out, "Samson! The Philistines have come to capture you!" When he woke up, he thought, "I will do as before and shake myself free." But he didn't realize the Lord had left him. So the Philistines captured him and gouged out his eyes. They took him to Gaza, where he was bound with bronze chains and forced to grind grain in the prison. (Judges 16:4–6, 17–21 NLT)

For 1,100 pieces of silver, Delilah betrayed her lover. She took advantage of the fact that he loved her and lured him into her trap. Somehow, we all have these kinds of people in our lives. They sometimes come to make us accomplish our purposes. Jesus had Judas, Samson had Delilah, Joseph had his brothers.

> It is not an enemy who taunts me—I could bear that. It is not my foes who so arrogantly insult me—I could have hidden from them. Instead, it is you—my equal, my companion and close friend. What good fellowship we once enjoyed as we walked together to the house of God. (Psalm 55:12–14 NLT)

We should keep in mind that these things happen, and when they do, we should not allow it to get to our hearts and we delay our destinies. Let's follow the example of our Master: "Don't let evil conquer you, but conquer evil by doing good" (Romans 12:21 NLT).

- Time to allow yourself to be broken so that you can be rebuilt.

> Very truly I tell you, unless a kernel of wheat falls to the ground and dies, it remains only a single seed. But if it dies, it produces many seeds. Anyone who loves their life will lose it, while anyone who hates their life in this world will keep it for eternal life. Whoever serves me must follow me; and where I am, my servant also will be. My Father will honor the one who serves me. (John 12:24–26 NIV)

Jesus used the kernel of wheat here to represent us. In other words, what Jesus is trying to tell us is that "except we die to ourselves (not physical death, but crucifying our flesh and its lustful desires, being broken …), we will remain by ourselves (trying to solve things by our own). But if we die to ourselves, we will produce many seeds (i.e. we will multiply in all aspects of our lives). Anyone who loves this life on earth (enjoying the pleasures of this earth) will lose it, while anyone who hate this life on earth (more concern about the things of the spirit) will keep it for Eternal life."

Jesus himself showed the example. So how do you know if you are broken?

> The acts of the flesh are obvious: sexual immorality, impurity and debauchery; idolatry and witchcraft; hatred, discord, jealousy, fits of rage, selfish ambition, dissensions, factions and envy; drunkenness, orgies, and the like. I warn you, as I did before, that those who live like this will not inherit the kingdom of God. (Galatians 5:19–21 NIV)

Apostle Paul said, "My old self has been crucified with Christ. It is no longer I who live, but Christ lives in me. So I live in this earthly body by trusting in the Son of God, who loved me and gave himself for me" (Galatians 2:20 NLT).

In this kingdom where we belong, things are different. We are called to share the suffering of our King, contrary to the world where kings and queens lord their authority over their servants and wait to be served. Matthew 20:28 (NLT) says, "For even the Son of Man came not to be served but to serve others and to give his life as a ransom for many.

The truth is, we can have all the glory that comes with our queenship on this earth, but it will be even more glorious after this life. "Yet what we suffer now is nothing compared to the glory he will reveal to us later" (Romans 8:18 NLT)

> So we don't look at the troubles we can see now; rather, we fix our gaze on things that cannot be seen. For the things we see now will soon be gone, but the things we cannot see will last forever. (2 Corinthians 4:18 NLT)

- Time to wage war.

> We are human, but we don't wage war as humans do.
> (2 Corinthians 10:3 NLT)

Yeah, there is time to wage war. One of the reasons I love King David is because he was a good soldier even though he was a king. He knew when to wage war and when to leave it in the hands of the Lord. We are in a constant war. There is a war going on in the spirit realm daily so that we should not become who God says we should be.

In 1 Peter 5:8 (NLT), it is written: "Stay alert! Watch out for your great enemy, the devil. He prowls around like a roaring lion, looking for someone to devour."

He is a thief who wants to destroy destinies: "The thief's purpose is to steal and kill and destroy" (John 10:10 NLT).

What do you do when someone wants to steal what belongs to you? Or when you know someone is plotting to kill you? Or you get to know that somebody wants to destroy your career and all the dreams and all you have been working so hard for? Do you run away? Leave it in His hands? Or you cry and try to negotiate? That is what cowards do, or people who are powerless. But as for us, power has been given to us. So there is nothing to negotiate; you neither sit down nor cry nor run away because even if you do, the devil has no mercy, no pity. He will still kill you and make sure you end up in hell.

> Finally, my brethren, be strong in the Lord, and in the power of his might. Put on the whole armour of God that ye may be able to stand against the wiles of the devil. For we wrestle not against flesh and blood, but against principalities, against powers, against the rulers of the darkness of this world, against spiritual wickedness in high places. (Ephesians 6:10–12 KJV)

What is the armor of God? (See Ephesians 6:13–18 AMP.)

Once you put on your armor as a soldier, you don't sit down and sleep with it. You go on the battlefield, on your knees. The adversary never sleeps, so we ought to pray at all times: "Be unceasing and persistent in prayer" (1 Thessalonians 5:17 AMP).

Any battle you need to fight is in prayer. Now it is important to let the Lord lead you in how to wage war to make sure you are not just making noise or just shooting in the air. Look at the example of David.

> Now the Philistines had come and spread out [for battle] in the Valley of Rephaim. David inquired of the Lord, saying, "Shall I go up against the Philistines? Will You hand them over to me?" And the Lord said to David, "Go up, for I will certainly hand them over to you." (2 Samuel 5:17–25 AMP)

There are times you will need to bind and loose. There are times when your warfare will only be in praise and worship as in 2 Chronicles 20:21–22 (KJV).

There are times when all you will need is to use the blood of Jesus: "And they overcame him by the blood of the Lamb" (Revelation 12:11 KJV).

Sometimes all you will need is faith. You just wait in faith that He is fighting.

> You won't have to lift a hand in this battle; just stand firm, Judah and Jerusalem, and watch God's saving work for you take shape. Don't be afraid, don't waver. March out boldly tomorrow—God is with you. (2 Chronicles 2:15 MSG)

Other times the Lord can just lead you to intercede and pray for others, as in Romans 12:14, 19–20 NLT.

Sometimes the way to win the battle will be to just obey, to submit to God and His Word: "Submit yourselves therefore to God. Resist the devil, and he will flee from you" (James 4:7 KJV).

Sometimes it can require a prophetic action:

> And the Lord said unto Joshua, See, I have given into thine hand Jericho, and the king thereof, and the mighty men of valour. And ye shall compass the city, all ye men of war, and go round about the city once. Thus shalt thou do six days. And seven priests shall bear before the ark seven trumpets of rams' horns: and the seventh day ye shall compass the city seven times, and the priests shall blow with the trumpets. And it shall come to pass, that when they make a long blast with the ram's horn, and when ye hear the sound of the trumpet, all the people shall shout with a great shout; and the wall of the city shall fall down flat, and the people shall ascend up every man straight before him. (Joshua 6:2–5 KJV)

Or sometimes you might have to do all of them at the same time. It's just to trust His leading. After all, it is not by our own strength but by His Spirit in us.

> What shall we then say to these things? If God be for us, who can be against us? (Romans 8:31 NLT)

• Time to learn and to love.

We said it before. As we go through all the challenges and trials and pains of this life, they all come to make us stronger and to learn from our experiences, whether good or bad. Everything we go through works together so that we can grow in knowledge and love.

> In view of all this, make every effort to respond to God's promises. Supplement your faith with a generous provision of moral excellence, and moral excellence with knowledge, and knowledge with self-control, and self-control with patient endurance, and patient endurance with godliness, and godliness with brotherly affection, and brotherly affection with love for everyone. The more you grow like this, the more productive and useful you will be in your knowledge of our Lord Jesus Christ. (2 Peter 1:3–11 NLT)

We all have a purpose, and going through that journey or going through the process is necessary regardless of your past or what reality shows you. Our confidence might be wavering and unstable, but our calling is not.

No matter what season you are going through, remember that the almighty King is taking you through the process of becoming a queen. Discouragement might come along the way, but do not give up. Keep your faith alive. Just like Ruth or Esther, everything you have faced or are still facing is working for your own good as you have been called according to His purpose. But also remember that some trials are just a way for the enemy to keep you in a place of stagnancy, and then you need to fight. May God give us the discernment of the different times and seasons of our lives.

So let us humbly submit ourselves to the beautification process that God has designed for us. Without it, we may never fully get to be the designated queen He called us to be. The process can seem long and painful, but it is for a great end, a great purpose. Even if we can't always see or understand what God is doing, we should just trust that He is taking us there.

9

The Beauty and the Beast:
A Queen Is a Worshipper

What a strange title, right? Believe me truly, I can't come up with this kind of title. I must have heard it somewhere. You might wonder what the beauty, the beast, and a queen being a worshipper have in common. But again I tell you, I would have asked myself the same question if I was the one reading. These words came to me in a place of worship. I heard them as I was talking to the Lord, just thinking about what He was doing in my life at that time and how He saved me from so many troubles. But especially how His love was transforming me.

I was surprised at how I was handling some of the situations that I was going through. I was actually contemplating the positive changes that had occurred in my character. You know, sometimes you are conscious of your bad character, and you are also conscious that it is not just bad for you but it's affecting your relationships. You want to get rid of it, but no matter how you try, you always find yourself in that place where you are sorry that you have that character. You really want to become better, but at the same time, some people around you will just do things that cause that character to pop up.

I shared earlier how I used to have anger issues, and it's still a daily process. It is not that I would get angry and break everything, but I used to get irritated so easily by little things and was always trying to be on the defensive, always ready to answer back. And sometimes when it happened at home (it mostly happened at home), my mother would just say in a funny tone, "That demon has come on you again." And we'd laugh. It always worked for that present moment. But I wanted it to last. I wanted to be a better daughter, a better servant. And though I am not married yet, I asked God to make me a good wife and a good mother. I desired not to just read what the Word of God says and preach it. I wanted it to be seen in my life. I remember I could give my mother a very hard time not only because of anger but other things as well.

When I seriously gave my life to Christ, I could see the difference in me. There was a change. At some points in my walk with the Lord, I could see more patience in me, more meekness and gentleness. But the funny thing was that when a really dramatic and painful situation arose, that was when I could see if the transformation was really taking place from the inside or was just superficial.

There was a situation at my workplace with one of my colleagues, and I was so angry. I mean so angry that I was scared of the anger I saw in me that day. Thank God, I didn't do anything stupid that day. I just went out to take some fresh air until I cooled down. But it made me see what was still in me. And that was years after I gave my life to Christ. I thought I was doing pretty well. I was so shocked because I knew that the Bible says that anger and rage are the works of the flesh. Obviously, I went to repent before God and asked Him to forgive me. And surely He did, as He always does. Was the character issue resolved? Not really. I prayed, I fasted, and I even cried to God to take out the evil in me.

A woman who considers herself from the kingdom cannot be identified with such things. So what was wrong with me?

We all know there are backgrounds, experiences, and environments that can cause bad or evil characters to develop within us. Psychology says that more than 80 percent of one's character and attitude is influence by the environment and genetics. We all have a story, whether it's from childhood, the environments we grew up in, the experiences we had, the trauma. Most of the time, that bad in us—what I call the beast in us—came from somewhere. Though it is good to identify where it came from, it's also very important to know how to get rid of it so that the fruits of the spirit, which are love (see chapter 4), joy, peace, patience, kindness, goodness, faithfulness, gentleness, and self-control can manifest within (Galatians 5:22–23).

Galatians 5:19–21 (NLT) says,

> When you follow the desires of your sinful nature, the results are very clear: sexual immorality, impurity, lustful pleasures, idolatry, sorcery, hostility, quarrelling, jealousy, outbursts of anger, selfish ambition, dissension, division, envy, drunkenness, wild parties, and other sins like these. Let me tell you again, as I have before, that anyone living that sort of life will not inherit the Kingdom of God.

So to continue with my story, I got to a point in my life that I was so weak spiritually and physically. It was a year full of drama for me, and I was so confused. I had done all I could—praying, fasting, spiritual warfare, sowing seeds—nothing. The only thing that I was able to do was worship. I felt so dry at that time. My bright smile was slowly turning to painful movements of lips. I would smile and laugh outside, but inside, only God and I knew what was going on.

After a while, God, in His faithfulness, did something great in my life that was comforting to my heart. And from that moment on, there was a turnaround. I could feel strength gradually coming back. I took some days of fasting and prayers, lying before the Lord, and rededicating my life to Him. From there, I cut down on my activities and decided to spend more intimate time with God.

Remember, I'm still dealing with my character here.

Then the Lord started showing me certain things: a little bit of unforgiveness here, a little bit of bitterness there, a little bit of envy here, a little bit of resentment there, a little bit of pride here, a little bit of malice there. Of course when God starts showing you your wrongs, you have to be open to accepting it and receiving the grace to change.

So I decided to go even deeper in Him and loving Him more by really spending time worshipping with Him. Time when I'll not be asking Him anything else but just acknowledging His greatness and holiness. Times when I will speak to him as a wife does with her husband. The more I was doing it, the more joy I had, more peace, more love for others. I started seeing things differently. My smile was brighter than ever before. Now, when I go pray or read the Bible, it is no more out of duty but out of love. In brief, there was real transformation taking place.

I didn't realize it at first. I could notice the joy and the peace, but when it came to my character, I didn't pay attention to what was happening to me. I was really deeply, excessively falling in love with God. And in His presence, I could feel the difference. He could calm the beast in me, and not only that, but also take it out gradually and bring out the beauty in me. Remember, I shared earlier that real beauty comes from the inside to radiate on the outside. To make the story short, that's how I came up with the title "The Beauty and the Beast: A Queen Is a Worshipper."

It was of Him.

The beast is the evil in us, the works of the flesh. The beauty is the Spirit of God in us, who we really are in Him.

It is in that place of intimate worship that you see the queen in you revealing herself slowly but surely.

I love to be in that place. It's a place where you can hear a still small voice that tells you the secrets of this life, that shows you the way to His heart, that tells you how beautiful you are in His eyes.

It's in that place where I write my songs and poems, where I get inspired, where I find strength and peace to go through the situations of life, where I find absolute joy. And where He can teach me to love just like Him.

There was a day after this real transformation started when I was reporting to God something that was heavy in my heart. It was actually something that I knew He wanted me to do, but it could be so painful because the results were opposite from what I was expecting. He wanted me to help someone, but the person could be so cold and negative with me. So I was telling Him with tears in my eyes and sincerity that it was too hard for me, and I wasn't sure if I wanted to do it. Then I heard Him tell me, "Do not do it for you or to please anybody. Do it for Me." As soon as He said, "for me," my tears immediately stopped, and I could easily answer Him, " Yes, Lord. If it's for You, I'll do it. Because I know how much You love me, and because I love You, I will do it. Just for You. Not even for what I could get out of it."

And many other things happened. I was surprised at how I reacted to them. Sharing love even with people who were mean to me. And all that because I was spending time in His presence.

In the place of intimate worship, you'll not see all these Bible instructions as bondage or restrictions. It will cause you to desire to go through the process of becoming a queen, not only on this earth, but to receive the crown of life once we get to heaven. Or don't you desire to see Him?

When a wife and husband spend continuous quality time together, they become more and more intimate. They start becoming like each other. The connection is very strong. The wife can easily tell her husband's mind and the same with the husband. They become one flesh. They are more in love with each other.

It works the same with God.

First Corinthians 6:17 (NLT) says, "But the person who is joined to the Lord is one spirit with him."

When you spend quality time with the King of kings, you start identifying yourself with Him. After all, the greatest commandment is, "You must love the Lord your God with all your heart, all your soul, and all your mind" (Matthew 22:37 NLT)

In this case, the beauty and the beast do not dance together. It's one or the other. They are always at war. When your beauty tells you to forgive and let go, your beast will tell you to pay back evil for evil.

As I mentioned earlier, another person I really love in the Bible is King David. Though he was a man, it doesn't change anything. I just want to make a point. King David was identified by God as "a man after God's heart." When I read the book of Psalms, I don't wonder why. He was a worshipper. Just take a look at Psalm 145. His written words show how deep his love and reverence for God were. Though he fell sometimes, he still stood up. That was part of his process. He was the youngest among his brothers, but when God was looking for the next king of Israel, David was the one chosen (1 Samuel 16). And even though he was anointed king at a very young age (some theologians say he was fifteen, others say seventeen, but that's not important), he only became the ruling king over Israel at thirty. From the time Samuel anointed him to the time David officially reigned over Israel, he went through his process. He never stopped worshipping even when he failed.

All this is to say that how much beast remains in you or how much beauty is seen in you depends on how intimate you are with God, the King of kings. A queen is a woman after God's own heart who makes worship the secret of her beauty. Worship here is not only in songs. Apostle Paul wrote:

> So here's what I want you to do, God helping you: Take your everyday, ordinary life—your sleeping, eating, going-to-work, and walking-around life—and place it before God as an offering. Embracing what God does for you is the best thing you can do for him. Don't become so well-adjusted to your culture that you fit into it without even thinking. Instead, fix your attention on God. You'll be changed from the inside out. Readily recognize what he wants from you, and quickly respond to it. Unlike the culture around you, always dragging you down to its level of immaturity, God brings the best out of you, develops well-formed maturity in you. (Romans 12:1–2 MSG)

The NLT version puts it this way:

> And so, dear brothers and sisters, I plead with you to give your bodies to God because of all he has done

for you. Let them be a living and holy sacrifice—the kind he will find acceptable. This is truly the way to worship him. (Romans 12:1 NLT)

So I pray we'll all be able to come to that place where we meet His love and desire Him earnestly and passionately. May we fall in love with Him. May we hunger and thirst for more of Him so that in our place of intimate worship, He'll take out the beast in us and bring out the beautiful queen in us. May we make a place in our hearts where He'll come to stay, and we'll cause Him to stay for always.

First Peter 4:8 (NLT) says, "But anyone who does not love does not know God, for God is love." For me, it's the same as saying, "Anyone who doesn't know God, doesn't know what true love is all about."

We should successfully fall in love with Him first, and then loving others will become much easier. You will also learn to love yourself even more.

The Learning Queen

"Study to shew thyself approved unto God, a workman that needeth not to be ashamed, rightly dividing the word of truth" (2 Timothy 2:15 KJV).

Can there be a queen without knowledge?

I'm not talking here about having the highest degree because degrees are not the only way to have a broad and vast education. There's a minimum that is required from a queen. There's a level of education we need to see in the woman or man who sits on the throne of a nation. You cannot lead from a place of ignorance, or you'll lead people and yourself to doom. Having read the biography of certain queens, namely Elizabeth I and Elizabeth II, Victoria, I realized they learned.

Queen Elizabeth I, for example, is so far recognized as one of the queens with the greatest education. By the age of fifteen, she could already speak and write six languages and had studied subjects such as math, geometry, history, grammar, philosophy, logic, and literature. As for Queen Victoria, it is recorded of her that she read about 150 works before she was seventeen years old. She read subjects such as history, religion, astronomy, and geography. Concerning the current queen of the United Kingdom, the one with the longest reign on earth, Queen Elizabeth II, she studied constitutional history and law as well as religion.

The Bible talks about studying to show ourselves approved by God, the King of all kings, the One who crowns us. It is for our own benefit and for those around us to rightly divide what is true from what is wrong.

The reason parents send their children to school is not because they don't have anything to do with their money. It's so the children will acquire knowledge that will help them to become something in life. If you noticed in the examples of queens I shared, they all studied history. Why is it important to notice that? The importance of history is that it informs you of what happened in the past, knowing that the past influences the present. It helps you to understand the events and changes that took place to bring us to the present society and environment. Queen Elizabeth II in particular studied constitutional history; that is, the origin and development of how the principles and laws of the kingdom were made and by whom. She also studied law, the practice of rightly dividing good from bad. One thing the constitution does is that it places in our hands the power of the government of the kingdom or the nation where we are. In chapter 7, I spoke about understanding the constitution and history of our kingdom. I said that the Bible is our constitution, so it is God's power in our hands.

One of the reasons you see a lot of Bible scriptures in this book is because I want to back up my words. In fact, I want to show I'm writing not from my understanding but based on the Word. Growing up, they used to teach us in our French classes that when writing essays, each argument should be backed up by a quote from a famous author or from the book we were reading at that present time.

This is to show the importance of reading the Word of God, the Bible. When the scriptures say to study to show yourself approve, it's in different fields but most important, the Word. Nowadays we have all kinds of doctrines circulating in our midst. I used to get so offended by those people who twist the Word of God and cause people to do all kinds of things. But now I blame us. I believe if you know what the scriptures say, you'll not be easily deceived. When you are dealing with lawyers, businesspeople, police officers, and all those who studied law, you can't fool them when it comes to what the law says. It should be the same with the queens of the Most High.

This is the story of a certain young man who lived with his father until he was of age to get married. He was a unique son to his parents. The mother had passed away a long time ago. The father never remarried and took care of his only son.

One day the young man traveled to a far country to attend to some familial duties. There he met a young girl who deeply pleased him. But she was evil and had no manners. She had a bad reputation and was known to all as "evil Gomah." But the young man loved her passionately. She was of an extraordinary beauty. When the young man decided to get to know her better, he realized how mean she was and how terrifying she could be. Yet while in that country, he never spent a day without going to see her.

Once he got back home, he told his father that he had found the woman he wanted to marry. The father asked questions about who she was and what she was like. The son was very honest with the father and told him everything he saw of the girl. Of course the father became very concerned with his son's decision. But when he saw how determined and passionate his son was concerning the young girl, he made a deal with his son before giving his blessing and consent for the marriage.

The young man went back to that country to spend more time with evil Gomah and show her how much he loved her. She was very resistant at the beginning, but seeing how caring, loving, and patient he could be, she started letting down her guard and allowed him to come closer. He was a very eloquent man and very charming. His humility and respect were beyond words.

After some difficult times with the young lady, she finally agreed to marry him and followed him to his own country. He had already prepared the place far from his father's house where they'd live together and set everything in place so that she would be at ease. The young man's family welcomed her in a very loving way. But the evil Gomah was so mean that it had become a nature for her. She tortured the young man so much, but sometimes she sat down and cried because she saw the pain she caused him. He was so patient. He knew she had fallen in love with him for real, and that it was only a matter of time before she would change.

And it came to pass after some months that the country was attacked by its surrounding neighbors, and a war was declared. As a soldier, the young man was called to go to war. So he left his wife, promising that he would send her letters every chance he could. About two months later, the war was still not over, but as he had promised, he sent Gomah lots of letters. At some point, she lost patience, and for some reason, she stopped reading his letters. She would not even open them anymore. As soon as she receive one, she will threw it in a drawer and forgot it.

As time passed and her husband had not returned, things became harder and harder for her. The women of her community hated her because the young soldier had chosen her instead of one of them. Some people deceived her by telling her falsehoods about her husband, which she believed. She was at a point abandoned to herself. She fell sick and had no money and nobody to help her. She started cursing the day she got married to the young soldier and said that had she known he was a soldier, she would have never followed him. She became so bitter, and in her sorrowful sickness, she died.

Just some days after her death, the young man came back and heard all that had happened. He fell to the ground and wept so bitterly because he loved his wife and was so eager to see her again. When the father heard it, he was also disappointed and heartbroken. He was concerned about his dear son. The young man gave her a befitting burial and mourned her for a good while.

After few years, on another of his numerous trips, he met a girl in the country he went to. She reminded him so much of Gomah. She was also just as mean and delinquent as Gomah was and also very beautiful; she had same traits as Gomah. And he fell in love with her. She was called Guiora. It seemed as if the story was repeating itself. He went back again to the father and told him he found another girl he wanted to marry. He thought he was given a second chance because he had thought that Gomah wouldn't have died if he was present. As you can imagine, the father was afraid for his son. He wondered why his son always fell in love with this kind of girl when there were beautiful and well-educated young girls around him. This time it was hard for the father, but after a while, he accepted the fact and made the same deal with his son before giving him his blessings for the marriage.

The young soldier married her and brought her to the same home he lived in with Gomah. He seemed to love Guiora even more and was even more tender and patient with her. Guiora also loved him, but she had been so mean that meanness became her twin sister. It was hard to get rid of it. But unlike Gomah, Guiora was more opened to receiving the young soldier's love. Because of his level of care and patience with her, she wanted to change; she wanted to love him back the way he deserved to be loved. But a few months into their marriage, he was again called to war! He was very sad and afraid that what happened in the past would happen again. He hugged his wife so tightly for a good while before he left. He promised he would write her letters every time he could. So he sent her letters on a regular basis. She was more and more impatient to receive his letters.

A few weeks after he left, he was badly wounded and in the coma for a while. When there were no more letters, Guiora became worried and sad. She was going through the same challenges Gomah went through and even more. The same people who deceived Gomah came to tell her evil stories about her husband. Some people even plotted to kill her. Then it came to pass on a fateful day, as she was cleaning the house, she happened to fall on the keys of the cabinet where Gomah kept all the letters she didn't read. The cabinet was in a guestroom in the basement. Gomah loved that cabinet, and it hadn't been opened since she died. So Guiora opened the cabinet and found all the letters. In her curiosity, she decided to read the letters because she realized they had never been opened. The first letter she opened read:

> My beloved wife, words are all I have for now to share my love for you. I am here, yet my heart is with you. But the thought of seeing you again keeps me alive every day and gives me courage on the battlefield. Things are not rosy down here, but to remember your smile is enough to enlighten my day. I can't wait to see you again. Before I come back there are things I need you to do, my darling. We'll be able to live our love with no limitations.

As Guiora read, she was amazed by the kind of heart her husband had. With everything she heard about his previous marriage and how he suffered, he wasn't afraid to love her, even though her character was almost the same as Gomah's.

So she continued reading. In another letter she read:

> Though I'm not present, I've arranged things so that you'll not lack anything. Please contact Mrs. August. I've written her number in my notebook, which I always keep in my car. It also has all the other contact information you'll need. Tell her you are my wife, and when asks you for the password, tell her, "You are my

gemstone," so she'll know I am the one who sent you. She will be there to help you and assist you. The choice is still yours. I'll understand if you want to do things yourself.

She realized that the young soldier was giving Gomah access to many secret things that he had. And every new letter unfolded new things. Since she was not receiving any letters, she decided to do everything that was written in those letters as if they were hers. He had planned everything—financially, physically (in case she was sick), emotionally, everything. In fact, Mrs. August was at her service, so she'd not have to worry for anything.

The more Guiora read the letters, the more she was determined to change for her husband. But was still worried that he was no longer sending letters. When she was done reading the letters, she was convinced that there was something different about her husband, and that there were things she didn't know about him.

After some weeks, she received a letter from her husband, who explained to her what happened and why he wasn't able to communicate with her. She was so excited. The transformation was evident in Guiora's life. And when the young soldier came home, he noticed that his wife had changed positively. He couldn't tell why. When he spoke with Mrs. August, she told him what happened, and he was overwhelmed with joy. So he went to his father's house and told him, "We got her!"

Confused, the father asked, "We got who? And what are you talking about?" The young man told his father all that happened in his absence and how his wife was another person, though she was not the best yet. The father couldn't believe it and decided to see it himself. He went to spend some time with them and noticed that at a certain hour of the day, she locked herself in the guestroom where the cabinet was. There she reread some of these letters. Though he wondered what she was doing, he couldn't ignore her transformation and agreed with his son. "I think you are right, Son. We got her!"

You might wonder what were they talking about.

Later on, the father invited them to his house. Guiora had never been there before. Every family member that she knew would come to her house and never took her to where they lived. As they got there, she couldn't believe her eyes and her ears. The young soldier she had married was actually the only son of the king of the kingdom where they lived. The deal the son had with his father was that as he was to be the heir to his father's throne, the woman who would become queen would have to prove she had what it took to be crowned queen. So they arranged for the son to live in one of the smallest villages of that kingdom, and nobody was supposed to tell her that the young soldier was the prince of that land. All the father wanted to see was if the woman was open to learning and to change. And that's how a delinquent became queen.

The reason I shared this story is because I wanted us to see the difference between two women: Gomah and Guiora. They were both wayward darlings who married a good man. If Gomah had opened her letters, she wouldn't have suffered and died the way she did. Everything was given to her. She just had to read the letters.

Guiora, on the other hand, though the letters were not really hers, spent time reading them. That's how she found out some secrets that led to other secrets that led her to the crown.

It is the same story with our God. You can be like Gomah and always make excuses for why you don't spend time reading your Bible, which were like the prince's letters. She died without knowing she had married a prince and that she didn't have to suffer the way she did. Or you can be like Guiora, who chose to read her way to her crown.

It's up to us. The Bible says in Hosea 4:6a, "My people are destroyed for lack of knowledge [of my Law, where I reveal my will]."

The Lord, the King, chooses to reveal unto us His will. That is the secret that leads to the crown. He reveals to you who He is in the Bible. He leads you on how to go through the same Bible so that people shall not come and tell you anything about Him and you'll believe it.

My dear queen, search the scriptures. Spend time reading His letters. That's when you'll realize His love for you, and you'll know what He is telling you. He'll tell you to go this way or that way; do this and don't do that for the enemy is waiting for you there; that's right or that's wrong.

Don't wait to hear prophecies or an audible voice telling you what is already written in the Bible. It is not for everybody. Don't be too lazy to read. Fight that spirit that doesn't want you to spend time reading so that you'll be ignorant and not know the truth. He knows that when you know the truth, it shall set you free from every bondage. That is John 8:32. Don't be a Gomah.

As for me, it's in the reading of the scriptures that I get direction. Sometimes I'll not be sure of what to do, or I'll be afraid to do what I have to do. But as I open His letters, He'll give me verses that will tell me what to do or not to be afraid.

The enemy has tried to deceive many, even the elected ones. It is the knowledge of right or wrong that will deliver us from his hands.

The Bible records that Jesus was tempted of the devil three times in the wilderness. The tempter used scriptures to deceive Him. He quoted Psalm 91:11–12 (that's in Matthew 4:6–7), and because Jesus was the constitution Himself, He is the living Word, He is the truth Himself, he answered with Deuteronomy 6:16a. We are not better than Jesus, so the tempter will come after us with scriptures used in the wrong context to deceive us. But a lady who studied the Word is worthy to be approved by the King.

So let your study of the scriptures take you to your crown.

So What?

I have racked my brain for a good moment and asked myself many questions as I was writing the book, and many things became so clear to me. The Father was showing me things, and I took time to examine myself. So now I would like you to think about these questions. And be honest with yourself.

The kingdom of God is as unto a man who sent his two servants into a far city to look for gemstones. Once they arrived in the city, they were received in the palace of the prince of that city. While one of them got caught up in different activities and feasts and services of the palace, still calling his master from time to time to ask for resources, the other one kept to his duties in the palace and went in search for the gemstones. Then it came to pass that at the appointed time, when the master went to bring back the servants and the gemstones they found, the one servant said to his master. "My Lord, the search has been very rough and difficult. The weather was not always pleasant. I fell sometimes and broke my legs and got wounded. Some other times I got burned by the sun but here is what you asked of me."

And the master answered, "Thou hadst done a good thing, thou hadst endured till the end of the race, thou shall certainly receive thy rewards."

Then the other one came and said, "Master, thou hadst always taught me to serve, to build, to be compassionate, and to help. So this is what I did. I helped the city to build bigger mansions, I served as much as I could, and I helped the poor. I was at every activity to represent you. See, O master, that I couldn't do everything together."

What do you think shall be the answer of the master to this servant?

Of the two servants, which one are you?

Do you believe in Jesus?

Do you believe He still saves?

Or do you think that He doesn't exist because of the many challenges you went through or saw others going through?

Or do you believe that all that you have is because you worked hard for it. and Jesus has nothing to do with it? Maybe yes?

If so, what gives you the assurance and the strength to wake up in the morning? Neither nature nor science can determine that. Haven't you heard of people who went to sleep and didn't wake up in the morning? Or don't you know of people who never smoked but ended up with lung cancer?

And at the same time, haven't you heard of people who were healed of cancer by Jesus?

If you still doubt that Jesus is alive and real, then ask Him yourself. It won't cost you anything.

Tell Him, "If you are real Jesus, then let me see how real you are."

If you believe in Him, do you know your identity?

Do you know who God says you are? Do you know you are beautiful in His eyes, even if other people say you are not?

Do you know you are the apple of His eyes?

Who can allow anybody to put His fingers inside their eyes?

He watches over you day and night, and He loves you. He wonderfully and beautifully made you, and even the devil knows. That is why he wants to kill you, did you know?

Are you conscious that you are a princess since birth?

Do you feel hurt, sad, rejected, and depressed? You might just be going through the process that all princesses have to go through in order to become queens.

Do you also know that some of the pain we go through, the heartbreak, and trauma, are caused by our wrong behaviors and that God has nothing to do with it?

Do you also know that even with that bad character or weakness of yours, He still loves you and wants to use you for His glory?

David was taking care of the sheep; Esther was an orphan; Ruth was a Moabite widow; Elisabeth was called barren; Mary (the sinner) was a prostitute; Rahab was a harlot; Zaccheus was corrupt, yet the Lord loved them and used them. Is there anything too hard for God?

Why are you discouraged by the situations of this life? Don't you know the story of Job in the Bible? Don't you know he had everything, and then the enemy, the devil, went against him, taking everything he had, right to his children. He afflicted Job with diseases and caused his friends to turn against him? Yet Job said, "though he slays me, yet will I trust in Him" (Job 13:15 KJV). Or don't you know that Jesus was wounded, despised, rejected, and crucified for sins He did not commit? He did them for us.

Will you allow yourself to go through the beautification process?

Don't you want to make heaven?

Don't you want to be at the Lamb's supper?

Can you examine yourself and know where you stand with God at this moment?

Can He count on you?

Do you make yourself available, or do you find excuses? How close are you to the Father?

Do you have a relationship with Him?

Do you love Him?

How much? Do you talk about Him?

Do you praise Him?

When Martha was complaining that her sister Mary was sitting at Jesus's feet to listen to what He was teaching rather than helping her in the kitchen, Jesus said, "Mary has chosen the good part." (Luke 10:42 AMP) Which part have you chosen?

Are you after His hands, seeking what He can give you or how much He can bless you?

Or you are after His heart, seeking to know Him more and to be more intimate with Him?

Or are you at His feet to listen and learn from what He is saying?

Are you afraid? Do not be. He said in John 14:27 (NLT), "I am leaving you with a gift—peace of mind and heart. And the peace I give is a gift the world cannot give. So don't be troubled or afraid.

> Do not be afraid, for I have ransomed you. I have called you by name; you are mine. When you go through deep waters, I will be with you. When you go through rivers of difficulty, you will not drown. When you walk through the fire of oppression, you will not be burned up; the flames will not consume you. For I am the Lord, your God, the Holy One of Israel, your Savior. (Isaiah 43:1–3 NLT)

Are you discouraged?

> This is my command—be strong and courageous! Do not be afraid or discouraged. For the Lord your God is with you wherever you go. (Joshua 1:9 NLT)

You and I can make it. We have to make it. We will not give up to the oppression of the enemy.

So can you just humble yourself and let Jesus lead? I may not have all the answers to your questions, but He does.

> The Lord is close to all who call on him, yes, to all who call on him in truth. (Psalm 145:18 NLT)

Trust in the Lord always!

Conclusion

We have come to the end of this book. In summary, we need to know that there is a queen inside all of us, and we belong to a loving, faithful, and powerful King who made us after His own image and likeness. So as He is, so are we (Genesis 1:27). We have received His Spirit, and because the Spirit of the Lord is upon us, we are anointed (empowered) to preach the gospel to the poor. He is sending us to heal the brokenhearted, to deliver those who are held captives, to make the blind—those who are lost, who do not see the truth—to see, and to set free those who are oppressed. It is now up to us to walk in the Spirit and not in the flesh, desiring/doing the evil things of this world.

Be a woman full of love. Like Queen Esther, desire to protect, reunite, humble yourself; be obedient, and ready to sacrifice your life for the kingdom's purpose.

Be a woman of faith like Ruth for it is faith that carried her through her journey. She had faith no matter the circumstances or what reality was showing her. There was a purpose, a crown for her ahead. She had faith to believe that the One who reigns in this kingdom of ours is who He says He is and will do the things He says He will do.

Be a woman of character. Character is who you are, especially when nobody is watching. Cut the gossip and quarrels and strife and jealously and backbiting. Share your weaknesses with other women of great spiritual maturity.

Be a woman of power, knowing that the greater one lives inside you, that you are more than a conqueror, more than victorious, He has made you heir to His kingdom.

Jesus died so that we can embrace our destinies, fulfill them, and have eternal life. That is not to say that there will be no challenges. But know that even when they come, we should brace ourselves.

> I have told you all this so that you may have peace in me. Here on earth you will have many trials and sorrows. But take heart, because I have overcome the world. (John 16:33 NLT)

And if you still think you are not worthy or that your character doesn't reflect that of a queen, go in His presence, seek His face. In the presence of the Lord, He will make you more like Him. He will transform you and shape you into His perfect likeness. You'll become His, and as you abide in Him, He will abide in you, and both of you will become one.

> And don't you realize that if a man joins himself to a prostitute, he becomes one body with her? For the Scriptures say, "The two are united into one." But the person who is joined to the Lord is one spirit with him. (1 Corinthians 6:16–17 NLT)

So as He is King, you will become a queen just like Him. Just stay in that place, that secret place, a place of intimacy. Just like in marriage, the more a husband and his wife spend quality time together, intimate time, the closer they are to each other. It is the same in our relationship with the King. Jesus is the husband; you and I are His wife.

> If you look for me wholeheartedly, you will find me. (Jeremiah 29:13 NLT)

If God could accept Rahab the prostitute; if He accepted Ruth, who spent her childhood in idolatry, doing what was evil in His eyes; and brought both into the lineage of Jesus (Rahab was the mother of Boaz and Ruth the great-grandmother of David), what then can't He do for you?

You were born to be a queen. Be strong and trust in Him. You are in the making. You are a light to this world.

For my single sisters, I invite you to read my next book, *Singles Sing Singles*.

Confession

If you have not yet given your life to Christ the Savior, want to come out of the kind of life that you are living, and want to be the queen He called you to be, please say these words:

> Dear Jesus, I come to You this day in all humility and reverence. I acknowledge that I am sinner, and I've been living in darkness all this while. Forgive me for my sins, for my evil lifestyle, and for all kinds of abominations I did in the past. I ask You to come in my life now, and I receive You as my Lord and Savior. Let your blood wash me clean and give me a fresh beginning. I love You and accept You in my heart right now. Have Your way in my life, take the lead, and deliver me from all evil Amen.

If you just said this prayer, I can only celebrate you and welcome you to the kingdom of God. You just made one of the best decisions of your life. My prayer for you now is that the Lord should keep you along the way and that his Spirit in you will help you to stand especially when nothing will make sense for you. Remember that the real fight is not with human beings but the devil. He knows you more than you think; so he knows your weakness and where he can he set a trap for you. Do not allow anything or anyone to come in between you and God. And I'll say it again, NOTHING! When you'll be heartbroken by certain things, talk to Him. Open your heart to Him and be attentive to his voice and to the signs.

He died for everyone so that those who receive his new life will no longer live for themselves. Instead, they will live for Christ, who died and was raised for them. So we have stopped evaluating others from a human point of view. At one time we thought of Christ merely from a human point of view. How differently we know him now! This means that anyone who belongs to Christ has become a new person. The old life is gone; a new life has begun! (2 Corinthians 5:15–17 NLT)

The seventeenth verse of that same chapter in the Amplified Version says,

Therefore if anyone is in Christ [that is, grafted in, joined to Him by faith in Him as Savior], he is a new creature [reborn and renewed by the Holy Spirit]; the old things [the previous moral and spiritual condition] have passed away. Behold, new things have come [because spiritual awakening brings a new life].

One Night with the King
(Continued)

The King

Who has believed My message?
I was despised and rejected, a man of sorrows, acquainted with deepest grief.
You turned your back on Me and looked the other way.
I was despised, and you did not care.
Yet it was your weakness I carried; it was your sorrows that weighed me down.
And you thought My troubles were a punishment from God, a punishment for My own sins!
But I was pierced for your rebellion, crushed for your sins.
I was beaten so you could be whole.
I was whipped so you could be healed.
Like a sheep, you strayed away and left the King's path to follow your own.
I was oppressed and treated harshly, yet I never said a word.
I was led like a lamb to the slaughter.
And as a sheep is silent before the shearers, I didn't open My mouth.
You didn't care that I died without descendants; I had done no wrong and had never deceived anyone, but I was buried like a criminal.
Because of this experience, you are counted righteous
For I bore your sins and interceded for you and died for you

(Based on Isaiah 53 NLT.)

The Lady

My husband lived.
My husband died.
My husband said He'll never leave me.
My husband promises me all His riches.
My husband calls me beautiful.
My husband is humble of heart.
My husband promises me heaven
My husband is good.
Yes He is.
My husband calls me the apple of His eyes.
My husband died to save me.
My husband, my husband.
My husband loves me; He told me so.
My husband wants me to come closer.
My husband seeks my attention.
My husband, O, my husband.
When I cheated on Him,
He still called me and told me He loved me the same.
He made me queen.
He knows I'm not perfect and full of junk yet.
He is always ready to forgive me.
My husband cherishes me.
He shares my cries and pains.
My husband is the best.
O, my dear husband,
I'm sorry.
I went for prostitution.
I neglected and abandoned You.
I am not worthy of Your love.
What?
You still love me even when people see me as an adulterer?
You still see me as Your beloved wife?
Tell me, who is your husband?

Can he be as mine?
My husband is unique.
He is the great I Am.
He is greatly to be praised.
He is my Lord.
He was, He is and is to come.
He is the Light.
He is.

The King

"Sing, My beloved.
Break into loud and joyful song, O My bride.
Fear not; you will no longer live in shame.
Don't be afraid; there is no more disgrace for you.
You will no longer remember the shame of your youth
And the sorrows of widowhood.
For your Creator will be your husband.
The Lord of Heaven's Armies is His name!
He is your Redeemer, the Holy One of Israel,
The God of all the earth.
For a brief moment, I abandoned you,
But with great compassion, I will take you back.
In a burst of anger, I turned my face away for a little while.
But with everlasting love, I will have compassion on you,"
Says the Lord, your Redeemer.
"For the mountains may move and the hills disappear,
But even then, My faithful love for you will remain.
My covenant of blessing will never be broken,"
Says the Lord, who has mercy on you.
"I will make your towers of sparkling rubies,
Your gates of shining gems, and your walls of precious stones.
I will teach all your children, and they will enjoy great peace.
If any nation comes to fight you, it is not because I sent them.
Whoever attacks you will go down in defeat.

But in that coming day, no weapon turned against you will succeed.
You will silence every voice raised up to accuse you.
These benefits are enjoyed by the servants of the Lord; their vindication will come from me.
I, the Lord, have spoken!"

(Based on Isaiah 54 NLT.)

The Lady

How I delight in my husband.
My husband can be your husband too.
I don't mind sharing Him with you
Because He loved you and I before we even chose to love Him,
My love and the reason I leave.
Jesus is the husband.

Singles Sing Singles

Introduction

Single girls, single boys, singles all the way. O what fun it is to sing great singles of the Way.
Single girls, single boys, singles all the way, O what fun it is to praise and bless His holy name.

Waiting on the Lord
For that one perfect soul mate.
Some looking for their Boazes.
Some looking for their Ruths.
Dreaming about that day
When they'll walk down the aisle.
What joy it is to sing and say
They both shall become one.

O single girls, single boys, singles all the way.
O what fun it is to sing great singles of the Way.
Single girls, single boys, singles all the way.
O what fun it is to praise and bless His holy name.

Praise His holy name, O praise His holy name.
For the Lord our God,
He is the One who will join you together with him/her, and no man shall put asunder.
And people shall sing and say,

"This is the Lord's doing."
And it is wonderful in our eyes.
Too much for our understanding.
A great mystery
For he who is joined to his spouse is one flesh with her,
And both joined to the Lord shall be one spirit with Him.

Singles girls, singles boys, singles all the way.
O what joy it is to sing great singles to the King.

Printed in the United States
By Bookmasters